ROUGHNECK
GRACE

ALSO BY MICHAEL PERRY

BOOKS

Danger, Man Working: Writing from the Heart, the Gut, and the Poison Ivy Patch

Montaigne in Barn Boots: An Amateur Ambles Through Philosophy

Population: 485: Meeting Your Neighbors One Siren at a Time

From the Top: Brief Transmissions from Tent Show Radio

The Scavengers

The Jesus Cow

Visiting Tom: A Man, a Highway, and the Road to Roughneck Grace

Coop: A Year of Poultry, Pigs, and Parenting

Truck: A Love Story

Off Main Street: Barnstormers, Prophets & Gatemouth's Gator

AUDIO

Never Stand Behind a Sneezing Cow

I Got It from the Cows

The Clodhopper Monologues

MUSIC

Headwinded

Tiny Pilot

Bootlegged at the Big Top

MICHAEL PERRY

ROUGHNECK GRACE

**FARMER YOGA,
CREEPING CODGERISM,
APPLE GOLF, *and*
Other BRIEF ESSAYS
from On and Off
the Back Forty**

WISCONSIN HISTORICAL SOCIETY PRESS

Published by the Wisconsin Historical Society Press
Publishers since 1855

The Wisconsin Historical Society helps people connect to the past by collecting, preserving, and sharing stories. Founded in 1846, the Society is one of the nation's finest historical institutions.
Order books by phone toll free: (888) 999-1669
Order books online: shop.wisconsinhistory.org
Join the Wisconsin Historical Society: wisconsinhistory.org/membership

Printed in USA
Designed by Percolator Graphic Design
20 19 18 17   2 3 4 5

Library of Congress Cataloging-in-Publication Data.
Names: Perry, Michael, 1964– author.
Title: Roughneck grace : farmer yoga, creeping codgerism, apple golf, and
    other brief essays from on and off the back forty / Michael Perry.
Description: Madison : Wisconsin Historical Society Press, [2016]
Identifiers: LCCN 2016025882 (print) I LCCN 2016036722 (e-book) I ISBN
    9780870208126 (paperback) I ISBN 9780870208133 (e-book) I ISBN
    9780870208133 (E-book)
Subjects: LCSH: Perry, Michael, 1964– Anecdotes.
Classification: LCC AC8.5 .P47 2016 (print) I LCC AC8.5 (e-book) I DDC
    814/.6—dc23
LC record available at https://lccn.loc.gov/2016025882

Thank you to the Wisconsin State Journal
for generous support of this project.

WISCONSIN STATE ▲ JOURNAL

To roughnecks who read and reflect.

And to Beth, with gratitude for getting me to the page,
and apologies for white knuckles.

CONTENTS

ROAD

CREEPING CODGERISM

FRIENDS AND RELATIONS

APPRECIATION

INTRODUCTION

The title of this collection arose from the subtitle of *Visiting Tom,* a book I wrote about my neighbors Tom and Arlene (Tom, on his own now, makes a few appearances in this book). I hoped pairing those two words might convey the idea of grace—given and received—beyond the purview of priests or perfection. That perfect things emanate from imperfect people. Based on my own character, I better hope so, from both directions.

It seemed natural, then, when I was invited to write a weekly column for the *Wisconsin State Journal,* to do so beneath the rubric of "Roughneck Grace." With each dispatch (most of them sent from a small room above my garage, but also from airports, motels, coffee shops, and more than once from a cell phone somewhere along westbound I-80) I try to attend to that second word as best I can, as I have long been allowed more grace than I've earned, including the freedom and opportunity to weekly write up a few hundred words about anything I wish.

As for the roughneck part, well, with these soft hands I'm hardly a deckhand, but I do try to draw from ground level. From the backyard, the back forty, the neighbor down the road. I often joke that I get my column ideas from my brothers, and indeed, this book provides plenty of evidence to that effect (although as you'll read, my brother John put a real crimp in my favorite dead cow story). I also frequently mine my own incompetence, a vein running rich, deep, and wide. The last time we compiled a collection of these short pieces (*From the Top*), a man approached me at a signing, pointed at the stack beside me, and said, "That's a great bathroom book!"

Humbly, I nodded.

HOME

MISSING THE PIGS

I miss the pigs.

For several years I raised pigs. I started with two. The following year I went to four. "Doubling the size of the operation!" I liked to boast down at the feed mill where the real farmers hung out. "Economy of scale, that's where yer profit lies!"

I specify "real" farmers because I am not one. Farm-raised, yep. And still live on a farm. But I make a living typing and running my mouth, and when you have hands as soft as mine you don't go around talking big about farming. Just as cutting up firewood with my mother-in-law's chainsaw doesn't make me a logger. Thus, when composing a brief biography for purposes of publishing and public appearances, I took to describing myself as an "amateur" pig farmer. I find it best practice to self-calibrate before others do it for me.

I sure enjoyed those pigs, though. Our farm had lain fallow for decades, and the day I turned loose my first pair of forty-pound feeders down beside the old barnyard, it felt as if the land livened up in recognition. I liked to keep the window of my writing room open so I could hear the *clankety-bang* of the hog feeder lids in the distance and detect the occasional happy barking grunt as the pigs chased each other around the wallow. For the next several years, to the signs of spring—robins, snowmelt, leaf buds—I added the sight of little pigs troweling their snoots through the dirt en route to becoming big pigs.

As pig farming goes, I did okay. It's tough to mess up a pig, really. Although one year I got carried away on saving money after discovering a secret source of expired bakery goods. We're talking a pickup load of hot dog buns (with a few donut boxes in the mix, which I'd squirrel away beneath the frozen peas in a chest freezer in the garage) for under twenty bucks. But all those cheap carbs created pork chops that were more fat than meat. I should have known better, having suffered the same effects after sneaking frozen donuts.

Now spring—or at least the uncertain early version of it—is here again, and I'm wishing for open window screens and the sound of pigs. But it's probably not gonna happen. I just walked out to the pasture and had a look around. Ragweed stalks are crowding the hutch where the hogs flopped in the shade. The fence is twined with dried wild cucumber and winter-stripped grapevine. The galvanized feeder is hidden in a copse of burdock. There haven't been pigs out here for a couple of years now.

The thing is, if you're going to be a good farmer—even a good *amateur* farmer—you have to get out among your animals every day. See how they're doing. Get to know their personalities, so you can pick up on the one that's not quite right, or the one that's limping, or the one getting squeezed out of the feed trough. A few years into my pig production phase, it became clear my writing and yapping were taking me on the road more and more—a welcome development, but not conducive to tarrying amongst the hogs.

So I changed my bio. Nowadays I am introduced as an "intermittent" pig farmer. Meaning, I hope to have pigs again one day. It seems a fine and accessible dream. No need to make a million or pull up stakes, and the infrastructure is still in place. Spring will come and the pigs and I will celebrate with a happy grunt, and—all things in moderation—an outdated frozen donut.

SLIPPERS

The younger child was taken ill today, and now after supper she is still on the couch, my wife having just read her a story and rubbed her feet. The sick bay is awash in books and drawing supplies and crumpled tissues and half-emptied mugs of tea gone cold. I can hear the soft voice of the tot as she murmurs to her mother, and I offer up the universal silent prayer of every parent, that the child might rest well and take what cures sleep will provide. Sometimes you feel yourself leaning toward sunrise.

For now, our family of four is quiet in the house, so quiet I can hear the *tick, tick* of the woodstove as the flames agitate its molecules, and the click of my laptop keys as I try to set this scene. The elder daughter is poring over homework in her late great-grandmother's recliner, an abrasively upholstered clunker that I can only assume was the pride of the furniture showroom floor for about five minutes in 1972. The chair matches nothing in the house but so perfectly conveys our memories of the departed matriarch that we can't imagine the place without it. It is also my second favorite nap chair, particularly right after lunch on winter afternoons, when through strategic positioning I can warm my balding head with the sun angling through the south-facing window even as the woodstove toasts my feet. (My favorite nap chair is an old green heap in my office above the garage. That one came from another great-grandmother, dates back to the fifties, and during cool, rainy spells kinda smells like it.)

While I normally write in the garage room, it's nice to be in the house with the rest of the crew on a night like this, just Dad on deadline, over here on the couch in the corner, wearing my reading glasses and slippers, contentedly un-hip (hip being something I never really was very good at, despite parachute pants and a righteous mullet in the late 1980s; any remaining hipness pretensions died for good right about the time I started loading diaper bags into a minivan—or perhaps even earlier, in my late thirties, when I first really got into all the chair napping). The slippers were a gift from my mother-in-law, given to me early in my marriage to her daughter. I remember peeling back the gift wrap and thinking I wasn't a slipper guy, but now I actually look forward to wearing them come cold weather, because if I'm wearing them I'm in the house, and things are settled and good. You don't wear slippers when you're on the run. I have one other pair in my office. Those are a gift from a kind reader, and I wear them only after I have put in my minimum daily mileage on the treadmill desk, yet another concession to self-preservation over style.

There are more sounds, each of a settling sort: The hum of the refrigerator. The rhythmic, watery dishwasher muffle. The low rumble from a pot atop the woodstove, filled with vegetable trimmings softening up in advance of being fed to our chickens, currently fluffed and roosting in the coop. The sounds are background and domestic, deepening the feeling that in this moment we—the family—are in communion despite our silence.

Beyond that, I have no grand pronouncement. No grand conclusion. No charge to offer, no punchy quip or goof to drop. We cannot know what the morning will bring. I hope the sick child will feel better. I hope my wife will wake feeling deservedly rested. I hope decades from now the teenager will remember a comfort in this the most unassuming sort of evening. Joy is elusive, and joy is fleeting. And yet—and this may be the premise of a riddle—those who chase it rarely catch it. Perhaps it is best pursued in worn slippers and old chairs, and best experienced not in some jubilant instant, but rather the most unassuming hour.

RELATIVITY

I came to parenting late. When my younger daughter turns eighteen I will be sixty. It's not a world record or anything, but it does kinda rearrange the ol' life plans—or brings into question whether there were any plans in the first place. I operate on the theory that this arrangement will keep me young, although early returns have been mixed. Just last month the youngster knocked on my office door and announced she was making house calls on behalf of a certain high-profile hair-replacement firm—apparently she viewed their commercials while watching reruns of *Bewitched* on a television channel aimed at an older "demographic" to which her father may or may not belong.

Even the fact that she is watching television calls my parenting into question. Our "watching" policy has fluctuated over the years from zero to a few hours a week. We don't have cable or the dish, and our internet doesn't support intensive online viewing, so that limits us to whatever arrives through the air. Our viewing also used to be limited by the fact that our only set was one of those VCR/TV combos with a screen the size of a hand mirror. But then as the result of a move we wound up with my mother-in-law's HD flat-screen and once Daddy saw the Packers on that thing there was some backsliding. In fact, Daddy tends to lead the decline. It is counterproductive to lecture your children on the evils of sloth and the tube and then have them come downstairs to use the bathroom at two a.m. only to find Dad slouched on the couch with nacho dust on his face while watching hair replacement infomercials. What I would like to say here is I am teaching the children about irony.

The other day when the school bus brought the young one to the mailbox there were tears. Some playground slight that carried over to home. In fact, it had been a rough week—one of those where you'd just like to huddle up and start over. As a parent you have this overwhelming urge to simply fix everything by creating a circle of safety within your arms. And of course that is the essential center of the endeavor. But even as you hold them you know you are letting go. That evening as I reached out to touch her brow after the final bedtime story, I found myself willing strength from my hand to her heart. But at the same time I was doubting my own strength. The thing you're never prepared for as a parent is the uncertainty in yourself. Have I done the right thing? How badly did I mess that up? What price will the child pay for my own incompetence or indecision? I wonder sometimes whether being an "older" parent is good or bad. There are times I see parents half my age doing twice the job.

In the end I know that all things are relative, and that even in our old farmhouse on a bad day we are living lives of privilege . . . and as a parent I will do my best to assure that my children understand that. I will also look in the mirror and recognize sometimes a guy takes himself too seriously. Last week the grade school engaged in a project that involved parental participation. I was proud and grateful to stand beside my daughter. One of her classmates ran up, and with a lovely smile asked, "Are you her grandpa?"

We've been giggling about that one all week.

TURKEY IN A DEER STAND

The turkey began to putt shortly after I climbed the ladder into my deer stand. It was early—a single star still winked above the ridge—and the tree branches were barely distinguishable against the predawn sky. The "putt" is a single sharp note turkeys use to signal alarm, and as I settled in to wait for light, the turkey repeated it steadily. I wasn't hunting the turkey, but I did my best to spot it as an exercise to sharpen the eyes. In short, I was honing my predatory chops. The sound was coming from above and nearby, somewhere in the surrounding canopy. As the light grew, the turkey continued to putt and I continued to scan the emerging treetops.

As do many of my fellow citizens, I spend a lot of time up a tree this time of year. Due to other commitments off the farm, we raised no pigs this summer and so I am especially keen on putting some venison in the freezer. Deer hunting is a part of my cultural heritage, stretching back through my direct ancestors to people I never knew, and since the time I was allowed to skip school in third grade to help my grandfather bring home a buck, I have never missed a season.

That said, I am hardly the deadliest of Leatherstockings.

For one thing, I rarely take to the trees without reading materials, or revisions and a red pen. When I should be replenishing my buck scent or checking the wind I'm more likely to have my nose in a book or reworking that tricky third paragraph. I once failed to take the largest buck I'd ever seen because he snuck up on my pine tree while I was reading Alexander Pope's *Essay on Man*. I find Pope's work chewy and was trying real hard to focus and as a result never saw the big boy approaching. When I glanced up, the buck was fifteen yards away and we were in direct eye contact. We played the stare game for a minute or so, but the instant I moved to set Pope aside the buck was gone. I was left with nothing but literature, which is not bad but makes for dry sausage.

Last week I hiked a fair distance to spend three hours huddled in a deep valley beneath a slow rain hoping to see a deer (this time I was reading *Poets & Writers Magazine* on my phone) before finally surrendering my post and trekking back up to the homestead just in time to watch a decent buck stroll up the blacktop driveway, hang a right at the garage, pass within ten feet of the woodshed, hop the sewer cap, and then cut across the garden before disappearing into the dusk.

As a youth I once tumbled from a tree stand in such a manner that I found myself dangling upside down in midair, saved from a fall thanks only to the fact that one of my feet had become wedged between the stand and the tree trunk. The memory was rendered especially poignant in that the cap on the bottle of buck scent in my left front shirt pocket was cracked, and the contents were dripping into my upturned left nostril.

Of course there is nothing funny about falling out of a tree, and these days I wear a safety harness. This protects me should I stop reading and writing and simply fall asleep. Sleeping is my single favorite hunting activity and terribly underrated as a means of attracting wildlife.

Daylight delivered itself, and I continued to search the sky for that putting turkey. The chirping was confoundingly close, but I couldn't spot the bird. Tree by tree I searched, blocking the landscape off in an imaginary grid, covering it block by block, keenly tuned to detect the slightest movement. After about twenty minutes of this, I tipped my head back and looked straight up, and there it was. With the right wind, that bird could have dropped an egg on my head. (Or worse, although once you've had buck scent up the nose, you really aren't moved by turkey scat on the stocking cap.) Point is, when it takes you half an hour of daylight to spot a turkey so proximally parked—and silhouetted against the heavens, no less—you are really underperforming as an apex predator.

Eventually the turkey flew off and I never did see a deer. But I got to watch the world wake up, and then I read the first half of a Marilynne Robinson essay exploring the idea of Calvinism and charity, and then my hands got cold and I went looking for coffee, which, as it turns out, doesn't grow on trees. Or at least not on northwestern Wisconsin box elders.

SUBZERO

I have just finished preparing for our first subzero night of the year. Nothing too complicated. Hung twin heat lamps in the chicken coop, where yesterday my wife added a layer of old hay from bales she toted home from the neighbor's place. I was on deadline, so she took the truck and fetched the hay while I was writing. My wife bucked bales on a crew in high school, and when she drove through the yard in that old four-wheel-drive truck of ours I marveled once again at the ways in which she has expanded my concept of the yoga instructor.

I hung those heat lamps high, well clear of the hay. First I had to run three extension cords end to end from an outlet in the granary, across the snow to a pigtail wired directly to a wall outlet integrated into the mobile coop (currently immobile in the snow). The pigtail is one of my rare good ideas—fortunately, my cousin (who understands that magick some call electricity) was available to install it and thus the coop has not burned down.

Next I installed a fresh battery in the tractor. The old one was deader'n a nail, as my people like to say. Actually, I just kinda wedged the new one in there as the mounting bolts have rusted solid and my fingers got too cold to finish the job. The tractor started, and after inflating a flattening front tire I was able to use the loader to lift and transfer assorted heavy objects (a barrel of sand, some concrete blocks, a length of railroad track) to the back of the plow truck for traction purposes. Next I cleared all the family bicycles out of the garage bay (it seems we won't need them soon), then backed the tractor in, remembering to drop the rollover protection system first, meaning I didn't rip down the overhead door, which when you function at my level of fuzzmindedness is no small victory. The tractor is my backup to the snowplow. Although I may not need it all winter, I park it here because while the garage is not heated, it is built into the side of a hill and rarely drops below freezing. Thus the diesel will turn over more easily, preserving that new battery. It is also better—in subzero or blizzardy weather—to have it accessible right here in the yard rather than in a snowbound, electricity-free pole barn down the hill.

Finally, I delivered a pile of fresh rags to the insulated doghouse where the cats stay and left the light on for the heat it would generate. After securing them with fresh food and water I went into the house to find that my teenaged daughter had stocked us with a big pile of firewood.

That night, after the rest of the family was in bed, I loaded up the woodstove, then sat to let the flames catch before I set the draft. The old house thudded and shuddered as the mercury dropped and the nails contracted. Cold is fine; cold below zero requires special measures. It was nice to think of the tractor stowed and ready, the plow set, the cats warm. From my seat before the fire I could see the square yellow glow of the chicken coop windows. Come morning it was twelve below and I had to stomp ice out of the chicken water tub, but there were fresh eggs in the nests. On the stiff walk back to the house I held one cupped warmly in each hand.

STILL LIFE WITH TIRE SWING

The sight of the tire swing hanging dead still at twenty below was an unexpected heart-whomper.

In fact it froze me in my tracks.

It was high noon and I had made a shirtsleeves dash for the house to prospect the refrigerator for leftovers. It was cozy up there in my room above the garage, and that first draught of outside air even *tasted* cold. Something to drink rather than inhale. Flows to the lungs like neutral spirits, with trace notes of rainwater and ozone. The sun had the countryside lit up Arctic-stark, the type of merciless shine that takes the breath from warmborn citizens who associate bright sun with vacation and beach blankets. There it is, blazing in the heavens, and yet we scuttle along with our shoulders hunched against the cold as if bracing for a blow.

But then I saw that tire swing, and I came to a stop. There was something powerful in the frozen motionlessness of it. The lower third of the rubber circle was fixed in the snow, and the bristly rope was drawn straight as a plumb bob to the limb above. The swing hangs from a giant white pine that—despite mutilations of windstorms and time—still manages stateliness as it anchors the yard. Even as I stood in the snowbanked trough of the sidewalk it didn't take much to summon the sound of laughing children running laps around the bulwark trunk as they waited to take their turn on the tire, dodging as a playmate swung a giggling arc through them.

My brothers helped me hang the swing during a weekend get-together shortly after we moved here. I steadied the stepladder for John, who is better at knots, while Jed hoisted and held the tire at just the right height. Then I drilled holes in the dependent half of the tire so the mosquito water could drain, and taped up the lower three feet of the rope like the handle of a baseball bat to protect small hands from burn or blister. All the while we worked, my elder daughter pogoed around us, bouncing her way through the impossible wait. When I finally lifted her aboard and sent her gently spinning, her laughter twirled through the air. Today that daughter is a teenager and taller than I, and right there is what threw the brakes on my lunchtime sprint: The sight of the snow-bound swing flashbacked me straight to the day we hung it, and while the distance from here to there—from now to then—is in theory a line straight as that ruler of a rope, it felt dramatically shorter and far more convolute.

Beyond the swing the granary was capped with snow a foot deep. The empty corn crib stood bare-ribbed against the back forty. Down by the barnyard, the blackberry canes arced up over and back into the snow like barbwire croquet hoops abandoned after October's final game, and from the stripped limbs of a back-valley maple came the *fee-bee* of an unseen chickadee. The air—as it always is at these temperatures—was infused with mortality. Everything was still, and nothing more so than that swing, a pendulum marking time without motion.

The thing about twenty below is it disrespects reflection and introspection. In short, overthinking leads to frostbite. I entered the house, made a sandwich, and ate it—an act of existential bravery that precipitated an immediate diffusion of mortality's tincture.

I then scuttled back to the garage, although not before stopping in the same spot for one more look. On sun-bright days such as this the sky can be so blue and the pine needles so green that if you tip your head back until the colors align just so, you can convince yourself it is summer, which we trust is coming.

BRAIN FREEZE

As I sprinted through the zero-degree night air clad in nothing but slippers, undershorts, and a Green Bay Packers hoodie, it occurred to me that this sort of behavior might disqualify me from delivering the *you're-not-leaving-the-house-dressed-like-that* lecture to the children come morning. But this was no time for second thoughts.

This deeply into winter, odd human behavior is standard human behavior. There is of course the popular notion of "cabin fever," a condition that persists even in the age of central heat and condominiums and drives us to do whatever it takes to break the hoarfrost boredom. From childhood I recall my siblings and I charging barefoot out the door and into the snowbound alfalfa field, the game being to see who could make tracks the farthest before dashing back to the house, our feet growing numb and then tender as they thawed. But if the redness in our cheeks was born of the chill air, it was also a manifestation of our exhilaration. The ubiquitous "polar plunge" springs from the same irrepressible urge to break free—if only for a breathless few moments—from the housebound season, with the added advantage that underdressed citizens might raise a few bucks for a good cause. I also suspect seasonal dyspepsia was the impetus behind the underappreciated sport of water-skipping, in which winter-blitzed snowmobilers cut holes in the lake ice and attempt to cross the open water (my first observation of this was in Chetek, Wisconsin, in the 1970s; attending the World

Championships in Siren, Wisconsin, remains an enduring high-light of my existence).

Still, it was not boredom that drove me to sprint for the chicken coop in my skivvies. Instead it was that other creeping winter lethality, laziness—specifically as it pertains to getting dressed. It isn't so much the cold we come to resent as it is all necessary preparations for the cold. The endless layering, the bulky swaddling, the lacing and tugging and zipping and wrapping and knotting—all the time-burning interventions required for a simple trip to the mailbox or to curb the recycling. We get so tired of tottering around like ear-flappered endomorphic mummies that we start taking sartorial shortcuts.

It doesn't begin with running starkers across the yard at midnight. It begins with stepping outside to start the car sans mittens. Or retrieving the newspaper in fuzzy slippers despite three inches of fresh snow. Perhaps you grab an armload of firewood without taking time to don a coat, or even a cap. You return to the house with an ice cream headache—a *hog pain,* we always called it—but it passes quickly, assuaged by the idea that your stubbornness stole back twenty seconds from winter, that time-suckiest of seasons. The postures required to walk underdressed through winter become ingrained: the hunching of the shoulders, the tensing of the neck, the holding of the breath, the clenching of the fists (the tucking of those fists into our armpits), the laser-like focus on thoughts of baseball, beaches, or baby ducks—whatever it takes to preoccupy the mind as ice crystals infiltrate our toes and cerebrums. We will do whatever it takes to shortcut the winter dress-up dance.

And so it was when I woke with a start at midnight last week and realized the chicken coop door was still open, exposing our precious layers to varmints that prowl without regard to the thermometer, that my first thought was not dismay over the idea of leaving my warm bed for the cold night, but rather grumpy impatience with the idea of getting all bundled up. Dressing and undressing for the trip would cost me more time than the trip itself.

You already know how I chose to roll.

When I lunged back into the house, the woodstove air felt water-bottle warm. In a trice I was deep beneath the blankets. I figure I stole a solid two minutes. I shivered happily. Outside, winter just sat there.

WHITE PINE DOWN

Mother Nature is a ruthless arborist.

Our front yard has been anchored—for decades long preced-
ing our presence—by a grand white pine. At its base the tree is
so large an adult and two tots can join hand in hand and barely
encircle it. Some of the overhanging limbs are so thick they could
stand as trees in their own right. The white pine has shaded
family picnics, served as home plate for wiffle ball and kickball
games, and my children have learned to identify our farmstead
from across the valley by picking out the tree's distinctive sil-
houette along the skyline. Not long ago I wrote how the white
pine's faithful support of my daughters' tire swing has created
memories that generate warmth even at twenty below.

Aesthetically speaking, the tree has been a tad on the gnarly
side for some time now, with gaps where limbs have died or
snapped in high winds or under heavy snow, or succumbed to an
attack of pine worms. One large limb has been serially cavitated
by a pileated woodpecker, making it look as if it has been strafed
with a large-caliber machine gun.

The last time a limb came off the pine, it hit the porch roof
and rumpled the rain gutters. That was two years ago, and ever
since we've had several family conversations (and one with our
insurance agent) about the fact that it might be time for that tree
to go, lest the next limb come through the bedroom window.

I was raised in a family of loggers. I can appreciate a tree in
the form of two-by-fours. As such, I have long maintained that I

am no tree-hugger. But I am a tree-sitter, a tree-leaner, and a tree-seeker. The trees may not speak to me, but I do cherish their deep-rootedness, and the way they reinforce my own smallness. And that yard pine of ours is as much a part of our home as the house and hills. So even though I knew it was time to bring it down—if only for reasons of safety—I dithered and delayed.

Enter Mother Nature, who in the wee hours this week took matters into her own hands, draping a quilt of white around the shoulders of our old white pine—and then just kept draping, until the quilt became a death shroud. I was in a motel room far from home at the time, but my elder daughter said the crash and thud came around two a.m., and come the morning our old pine looked like it had been pinched and stripped, morning sunlight pouring through it in all sorts of new places. The biggest of the limbs were snapped in a manner belying unthinkable physics, and (although the younger child might not agree) we're grateful that the swing set was the only thing crushed.

When I returned home, it was a startle to come around the last curve of the driveway and see that tree . . . or what was left of it. I'll admit to a pang, and it will take a while to reprogram the visual elements of our sense of place. But close on the heels of my sadness came a sneaking sense of relief when I realized that Mother Nature had excused me from any more mushy-minded muddling over the fate of that tree. Come spring, the remains will simply have to come down. We won't be able to do a lot with it—some of the upper limbs will warm us as firewood, but you can't do much with a yard tree after generations of kids driving treehouse spikes and other saw-wrecking unknowns into the trunk.

But I'm grateful it went down this way. There is something honorable in the idea of the snow—of nature—claiming that tree, rather than the chainsaw. It is as if it has been allowed, after all these years of service, to, if not go out on its own terms, at least die a natural death.

REAL WINTER

This is that stretch where you gotta hunker down. Winter is given a pass—even welcomed—from mid-November through December because we're all hoping for a white Christmas, and any cold and snow that does arrive is diffused by colored lights and holiday hustle. December's winter is greeting card winter. In fact, we're disappointed if it doesn't arrive on schedule with Santa.

January we can handle because we're still running on pride. Whatever January throws at us, however deep the snow piles or the mercury drops, we bundle up and angle our bodies in the posture of perseverance. This is not a season, this is a character test. Chilblains and blizzards come with the territory; we are not deterred. Hand me that shovel, drop that plow, scrape that windshield, we're gonna make it.

By mid-February you catch yourself checking the darkness against the clock. Two months ago you cut a clean path to the garage in the spirit of an explorer charting fresh frontiers; now you push and peck your way through the drifts with all the verve of a groaning robot. The adventure is a chore, the snow shovel is five pounds heavier and seems to catch on every concrete crack. This is the time of year when you enter "s" into the online search field and it autofills with "seasonal affective disorder." The delivery vans that only weeks ago were on their pell-mell holiday runs stop-and-start more sparsely now, their Christmas cargo replaced with mail-order photo-therapeutic light boxes. This is the stretch of calendar when you can raise money by cutting a hole in the ice and inviting underclad humans to jump in. The motivation here is usually a good cause; it is also the desperate search for any sort of revivification, even in the form of breathless shrieking.

As I write this we have had an early thaw. The driveway is slushy and for the first time this year I can see bare blacktop again. But I checked the extended forecast, and within forty-eight hours we're going subzero. The slush will solidify into rock-hard lumps and ridges, just the thing for your funny bone or a hip pointer when you misstep while spreading salted sand from a soup can.

Few things are more disheartening than a below-zero stretch following melt. What was once a winter wonderland now has all the appeal of a pail of refrozen ice cream. All the creaminess is gone, replaced by crystal and grit. You find yourself—against all sense—hoping it will snow again. February? That's the month you start making deals with the weather gods: *New snow, please? To cover the old snow? Or some sun, please? Ten below, okay, three days straight, but please, at least a blue sky? So I can look straight up and* pretend *it's warm?*

We still get snow in April. May, even, is not wildly unusual, and thus I leave the snowplow attached. Spring snow and cold snaps are setbacks, sure, but by that time your soul has been rehabilitated by light. The darkness has ebbed, you feel the warmth winning. Here in February, the ratio has yet to hit the tipping point.

There is another month, of course: March. Sometimes March is April. Sometimes March is January.

Here in February, we do not talk about March.

SPRING MELT

Finally spring is here. Which is to say, lately the snow has been mixed with rain.

And yet even as the soggy snowflakes plop, there are signs that the season is shifting. Along the south side of the granary the first nubs of rhubarb are nosing through the muck. The mornings are filled with the sound of songbirds having second thoughts. And there is fresh water in the basement.

Although we live on a hill and are blessedly spared any immediate concerns about large-scale flooding, we do have our trouble spots, the basement being chief among them. Constructed of large rocks and gaps in the 1880s, it is a testament to persistence, strong backs, the pioneering work ethic, and the fact that they never really thought about putting a ping-pong table down there. In fact, when I descend to fetch a jar of canned beans or put the sewer snake through its paces, I have to keep moving so as to avoid mildew of the ears. My wife has looked into and obtained quotes for various preventive interventions ranging from drains and sealants to backhoes and home equity loans and I have been cornered and forced to look at brochures, but so far I have managed to save us money by putting off any decisions until mid-winter, when A) the basement is freeze-dried, B) it's too cold to stand down there talking about it, and, C) our concerns have shifted to the parlous state of the plumbing.

Another perennial water management challenge presents itself in a stretch of our concrete sidewalk that was apparently poured by a distractible contractor suffering from an inner ear problem and froth in the bubble of his transit level. After a pretty good run from the driveway to past the doghouse, just beyond the spirea bush it dips into the earth like the backbone of an over-loaded mule. This allows it to collect spring melt until it becomes a navigable waterway on the order of the Erie Canal. One finds himself splashing along humming a Pete Seeger song.

Naturally the worst stretch is right in front of the porch steps. Unlike with the basement leakage, however, I have taken decisive action to counter the swamped sidewalk: rather than force guests to navigate the path by supplying, inflating, and poling their own raft, I have placed two wooden pallets in the deepest spots, ar-ranging them in such a manner that with only a skip, two hops, and one teeter, they can grab the railing and pull themselves drily to safety and dinner. When someone in our household and my marriage dismissed this as a "temporary" solution, I harrumphed and pointed out that it's been working fine for six years now and furthermore those pallets are made of treated lumber and should last forever. The only downside being that someone might catch a heel between the gaps in the boards and do a half gainer into the flower bed slush, but then as you might have inferred by the description of our basement and our sidewalk, we don't have a lot of guests showing up in heels.

And so we wait. Through the rain, through the snow, through the melt, through the freeze and refreeze and un-refreeze, through the seasonal come-and-go. In a younger, more poetic age, I once described spring as treating us to a "titillating dance of veils." I have since come to think of it more as snapping us on the butt with a damp towel while tracking mud around the house, leaving the refrigerator door open, and letting the bathtub overflow.

One longs for daffodils. And a sump pump.

MAKING THE MOST OUT OF MOLES

In San Juan Capistrano spring brings swallows. Here we get moles. The furry kind, that is. The furry kind with four feet that tunnel through the yard, that is.

Something must be done. I am aware, after the requisite on-line search session, that there are innumerable alleged ways to get rid of moles and thus to broach the subject is to beg for a heavy-duty swamping of the in-box. Penetrating traps, insecticides, fumigants, subterranean metal barriers, improved soil drainage . . . or my favorite bit of advice: "Simply wait it out . . . moles live less than three years."

Um, unless that's a celibate mole, I call foul.

What we are admitting here is that up to and including a nuclear holocaust, the moles win and will party with the cockroaches. So perhaps instead of treating the yard, setting the traps, and hoping for insectivore abstinence, a guy might just go with it, and start a mole farm. Clearly conditions here are perfect . . . right from my room over the garage I can see a network of willy-nilly ridges crisscrossing the property as if lain out by a highway engineer raised in a pinball machine. And that's only the yard—I've got another thirty-seven acres to work with. Imagine the burrowing herds.

The greatest challenge, of course, will be marketing. For starters, the mole is not so photogenic. The paddling claws, the narrow snoot, the teensy eyes; it's tough to overcome the prejudice of prettiness. Right out of the gate it occurred to me that a market might exist for the pelts. After all, an English queen once tried to reduce Scotland's mole population in this very manner by popularizing moleskin coats, but she was a queen and her resources were beyond mine, and besides, who's gonna tell the queen her coat resembles the third cousin to a rat? Plus, I looked into the matter and it takes something like three thousand pins to hold all those teensy mole pelts together while you sew them up, and clumsy as I am that just sounds like the sort of thing that leads to outrageous medical bills.

I gave further deep consideration to the possibility of promoting moles as an unexploited source of protein. I have some preparatory experience in this area as I once very nearly made a million dollars selling surplus squirrels in the form of jerky (or, as I called it: Squerky!™). Sadly, the dream died when I was unable to attract the requisite angel investors. Sometimes people are blind.

I suppose the key is to pitch my moles as "pasture raised," which is sorta true except they dine mainly on grubs and earthworms, which is tough to frame. I'm seeing tiny artisanal sandwiches, marketed as "Pasture-Raised Mole on a Roll." Or a hearty salad: "Mole in a Bowl." Shish kebabs? "Mole on a Pole." Or perhaps the key is to follow the lead of the folks who renamed the Patagonian toothfish to the much more poetically palatable Chilean sea bass. Rather than convince people to enjoy minced mole I'll offer Loin of Lawn Tunneler, or Subterranean Sirloin.

Or I could simply hire a bulldozer, shave off a foot of topsoil, and start over. Because tomorrow morning there will be fresh tunnels. And somewhere in there, the responsible party, a mole, enjoying the first earthworm of spring and dreaming of love, no matter what they say.

PHEASANT LOVE

The day was fresh as only early spring mornings can be. The sun was bright but callow in its warmth, as if the shirtsleeves feel could be swept away by a single chill breeze. The first flecks of pale green had appeared on the lilac branches, and over by the granary the rhubarb was emerging. I had just fed and watered the chickens and was crossing the yard toward my office in the room above the garage when I heard a commotion. The garage is built into a hillside, and the noise—a general stirring of leaves and snapping of twigs—at first sounded like squirrels tussling, but then two male ring-necked pheasants broke into the open, one hot on the tail of the other.

It's not uncommon to hear the rasping squawk of these fellows out beyond the reaches of our yard, and now and then a solo rooster will skirt the perimeter over where the spruce trees line the pole barn, but this was the first time I'd seen two males in such close proximity. Their iridescent green heads and blood-red masks were startlingly beautiful as always, but in this case they were moving low to the ground in a dead-on sprint, the rearmost rooster pecking at the tail of the front-runner.

I had seen no hen, but her presence was implied, and although I don't speak pheasant, the message the pursuing rooster seemed to be conveying via his agitated clucks and snapping beak was that this was not going to be an open relationship. As for the rooster in retreat, his dedication to heading down-country in all due haste implied that he had gotten the worst of it back there behind the garage and was now engaged in what the great Patrick McManus once described as a "full-scale linear panic."

Having burst into the open, faced with nowhere to hide, and unable to outrun his jealous pursuer, the lead pheasant took to wing.

The second pheasant launched right behind him.

Their trajectory was such that they were headed straight for the face of our big red pole barn. Maintaining a small lead, the lead fleeing pheasant pumped his wings extra hard and cleared the roofline with a foot to spare. Right behind him the second pheasant flew smack into the corrugated face of the shed.

I mean, it wasn't even close. Missed clearing it by at least two feet.

He flapped and spiraled to earth, flopped on the bare ground, then scrambled to his feet and wobbled in a circle.

I laughed out loud. I didn't intend to be cruel, it was just that the whole scene was so unexpected, and so goofy, and to see that bird go from defending his love at warp speed to bending his beak against a steel shed the size of a two-story car ferry—well, let's face it, my history is such that the image conjured memories of my own romantic metaphorical equivalents.

Eventually, the bird fluffed his feathers, hopped nimbly through the fence, and disappeared into the brambles in a direction suggesting he was feeling much better and circling back to the place from whence he came.

Which was when I realized: I may have had a laugh at his expense, but the altitude-impaired pheasant did manage to run his competition out of contention and was now headed back to his sweetheart. And while the skedaddling pheasant cleared the barn and made a clean escape, he was now out there in the back forty weeds all alone.

Love is difficult.

FIXING UP THE COOP

Events have been placed in motion. Somewhere out there a box of fuzzy chicks is inbound. They will arrive teensy and peeping but in short order will be full-feathered and looking for lodgings. Our current batch of layers (fifteen of them, plus Goldie, who hasn't produced an egg in years but skates on charm, seniority, and the long memories of young children) resides in a classic little outhouse-looking coop, and if we try to cram in the new arrivals there will be cohabitation frustration, poultry pouting, and likely some busted eggs.

And so it is time to resurrect the larger coop. I say resurrect because currently it is parked in the weeds out back beside the septic mound, has one flat tire and one busted door, and requires a thorough cleaning followed by six coats of paint. I may also have to evict one woodchuck.

I will inflate the tire using the portable air tank I repaired last week by replacing a faulty valve. The way I strutted around after completing this simple fix is a sad and accurate testament to the low bar I set for basking in any sort of mechanical success. (Made it halfway through a Beginner Level Erector Set before dissolving into tears? Victory!) I was additionally buoyant having been given an excuse to swing by Farm & Fleet in order to purchase my own personal valve stem wrench. Joy is where you find it.

Pulling the coop from the weeds should be a simple proposition as it is mounted on the running gear from a hay wagon upon which I used to stack hay bales as a youth. Pulling it into the pole barn where all the tools and lumber are will be a more difficult proposition as I will have to spend three days clearing out the pole barn, excavating the workbench, and figuring out I don't have any of the lumber required.

And then the tough part: Actually repairing the thing. If my mechanical skills are poor, my carpentry abilities are even worse—you will get the approximate idea if you close your eyes and imagine a man attempting to play with Lincoln Logs while wearing oven mitts. Add tears, mingle with curses, beware flying hammers.

Oh, it promises to be quite a cobble job. And all the while, those chicks—peeping and fuzzy at first, but growing real feathers and clucking impatiently as they grow into chickens in need of housing—serve as an implacable deadline. But my teenaged daughter has asked to help me.

Asked.

Do you know how light that made me in the heart? The night the coop on wheels was finished by my cousin Ivan the carpenter (you thought *I* built it?), that same daughter—in grade school then—and I camped out in it overnight. The floors were still clean and smelled of pine. We giggled and made jokes about being chickens. Since then the coop has housed legions of actual chickens, received thousands of eggs, and then been mothballed. Meanwhile, the little girl who giggled in the coop has grown into a young woman and will be taking driver's education courses this summer.

I don't know how fixing up that rolling chicken shack will go. Based on prior experience there will be a lot of measuring twice, cutting once, then cutting again, and then maybe slathering a seventh coat of paint over the rough patches. I expect there will be some bent nails. But here is my parent's prayer: Long after this latest batch of chicks are lost to history, long after the daughter is grown and gone, long after the coop is flat-tired and weathering in weeds again, the state of repair will be secondary to the state of any memories hatched as we hammer.

EASTER

By now the Easter eggs—nearly all of them—will have been found. I say "nearly" because there are always those stragglers, the ones you discover with the lawn mower, or while vacuuming behind the piano, or after three days of trying to figure out where that smell is coming from.

During my bachelor years, the annual Easter egg hunt dropped off my radar, so it was a throwback the first time I stepped through my own kitchen door as a family man to discover the table draped in pages from the weekly shopper and ringed with children kneeling on chairs as they dunked and decorated eggs. The scent of warm vinegar, the copper wire dippers, the dye tablets, the scattered cartons, it all brought back my own memories of doing the same thing at their age. I joined in and colored up a few eggs myself. I found I still enjoyed the simple trick of writing on a plain shell with the clear wax crayon only to have my scribbling magically appear when I pulled the egg from the cup. I also discovered I was still too impatient to get richly colored eggs; as I child I nearly always pulled them too quickly and wound up with a series of anemic pastels.

These days our Easter egg sessions include a growing contingent of cousins. A few of us grown-ups hide the first eggs during breakfast, when the children are distracted. If weather allows, we place them all around the yard and outbuildings and in flowerpots and the lower-level branches of trees. When the porch door opens, you want to be well clear, lest you be trampled by a stampede of small feet. They fan out across the yard, yelling and running willy-nilly, leaders and followers, some of the older children holding back out of politeness, others motoring right past just because they can. As with any annual event, this is also a time when we mark signs of time and transition: the child that a few short years ago toddled along with his basket held high above his head to keep it from bumping the ground now has height enough to run along with it hanging freely from his hand; the preteen crosses the yard on a wavering path, vacillating between excitement at spotting an egg and self-consciousness at picking it up.

There are always some tears, maybe from a tumble in the flower bed, or a basket upended, or an egg underfoot, and in addition to the comforting, we parents always have to do some refereeing, especially if an older kid is poaching all the obvious spots. But the sounds that echo into the valley and its bare budding trees run heavily to happy.

Here on the farm, our outdoor Easter egg hunts take place within full view of the chicken coop, and I wonder sometimes as I see the hens, heads cocked at all the action, what it must be like for them to see the landscape strewn with eggs of every stripe and color. And then I watch my younger daughter, scampering joyfully hither and yon, chucking egg after egg into her brightly woven basket, and I think of the contrast come Monday, when she will approach the coop with a much plainer wire basket, the skip in her step toned down to a trudge as she does her after-school chores, the fun faded and eggs just plain old eggs again.

DEER REUNION

This morning as I stepped out of our farmhouse I was nearly run over by a white-tailed deer trip-tropping up the sidewalk. She passed so very near that I heard her breathing, and so preoccupied was she that she didn't even notice as I pulled up short on the steps. She crossed the yard in a worried zigzag, ears pitched forward. Every now and then she would stop and issue a curious noise somewhere between a croak and a wheeze, after which she would duck her head in all directions, staring intently as if awaiting a response. Earlier today my daughter and I had seen a doe and fawn at the far end of our driveway. Whether or not this was the same deer, it seemed clear she was searching for her fawn. After ducking beneath the volleyball net, she jogged around behind the pole barn and out of sight.

Deer are hardly a rare sight around these parts, and one certainly need not live at the far end of a dead-end road to participate in close encounters like this. Last year a friend of the family spent an entire day freezing and seeing nothing in a deer blind deep in a two-hundred-acre forest adjacent to our farm only to have to stop traffic a block from his suburban home in order to let an eight-point buck lead a clutch of does past a fire hydrant and across the road before ducking behind the neighbor's garden shed. The following day the man froze in the woods once more, and again saw nary an antler until he returned to town. This time he texted me with a photograph attached; the buck was standing proudly on the boulevard beneath a sign reading

SPEED LIMIT 25. Nonetheless, I felt privileged to have happened out the door at just the right moment, and to have been privy to the uncommon sound of the doe's voice—a call far rarer than a buck's love-struck grunt, which can be heard any autumn.

After the doe disappeared, I went about my morning, slightly preoccupied by her unsettled demeanor. I couldn't help but feel some parental angst: What must it be to become separated, and to rely on the fates—and limited language at limited volume—for your safe reunion?

An hour later I had returned to the house and was stepping out again when the scenario repeated itself. The doe—the same, I assumed—came trotting through the yard from the opposite direction, oblivious to my presence on the porch steps. She was still uttering the same call, pausing every twenty feet to swivel her ears and listen. She tacked across the lawn and past our granary and was beside the corn crib when she stopped dead and looked to her left, peering intently into a fringe of tall grass encircling a stand of spruce. And then, as I watched, a fawn came bouncing out of the fringe, ducked beneath the doe's outstretched nose—*No time for kisses, Ma, I'm starving!*—and headed straight for what would now be brunch. In short order the fawn's bright white tail was flipping back and forth like a fuzzy windshield wiper, a semaphore for joy if ever there was one. I stood stock-still for a long while, loathe to interrupt either the reunion or the meal. When the fawn finally detached to touch noses with its mother I took a few steps toward the garage, a movement that sent the two of them scampering off behind the pole barn. And so we parted, me to do my human things, they to do their deer things, each of us feeling a little better about the day.

HAYSEED

I have just walked the trail along our ridge, and it looks as if the timothy is about to head out. Which is not to say a boy named Tim is about to depart, but rather to say one of my favorite perennial grasses is about to ripen. Whenever I pass by a head of green timothy, I tug at it. It's a reflex going back to the days when I was a farm boy no taller than the timothy itself. If the plant is young, and you draw at the head—composed of spikelets raspy as a cat's tongue—with steady pressure, the stalk will suddenly give and slide tightly from the clasping leaves. The butt end of the stalk is moist and tender, and I take small bites with my incisors—*nip, nip, nip*—and chew the bits, which taste like a mild celery.

After biting the tender part away (about an inch in, the stem becomes tough and fibrous) I discard the stem by tossing it like a miniature javelin. The fat head serves as fletching, and the effect is relatively aerodynamic, allowing the stalk to fly through the air on a clean arc. Late in the season it gets harder and harder to find plants with tender ends, and often the stem snaps in two rather than sliding neatly out.

The stalk also fits nicely in the space between my two front teeth (I am the proud owner of a professional-grade diastema), and I'll bracket it there, flicking the stem end with my tongue so it bounces against my lower lip, the stem flexing like a super light tackle fishing rod. This is your classic hayseed pose, and I find it useful in focusing the mind when some pondering is in order.

During my walk, I also noticed that the goldenrods are becoming tumorous with galls. The galls—each a swollen globe roughly the size of a filbert—always remind me of the winter we first harvested them for my grandfather. The only thing Grandpa loved more than fishing itself was trafficking in fishing intelligence ("I got a real hot tip," he'd say) picked up from reading *In-Fisherman* magazine, in conversation at the boat landing, or while eavesdropping general bait-shop scuttlebutt. Whenever he drove up from the city with his motorboat or ice fishing tent he'd assure whichever lucky grandkid was accompanying him that day that the fishing trip was a guaranteed success thanks to some insider info on the latest killer lure, the latest limnological fluctuations, or the latest undiscovered lake (always, for the sake of secrecy, referred to as "Gunnysack Lake"). One winter while kibitzing over some other guy's ice fishing hole, he was told that within each goldenrod gall there resided a worm that fish found to be irresistible. When he showed up at the farm with this news, we kids were only too delighted to take him out back and direct him to the fence lines where the brittle goldenrod stuck up through the drifted snow. We snapped off several handfuls, avoiding those already bored by woodpeckers, and later in the house when he halved them with his jackknife, sure enough, there was a small white grub encased within. For several years after that, we packed glass peanut butter jars full of galls and gave them to Grandpa for Christmas. This time of year the galls are still the color of miniature green apples, but later in the year they will blush apple-red. By the time the first snow arrives, each nut-sized globe will have turned a burnished brown, and the larva will be juiced with its own antifreeze, hoping to survive to spring, when—if it has been overlooked by woodpeckers, chickadees, and the grandchildren of ice fishermen—it will emerge as a fly and enjoy two weeks of life and love.

But I am getting ahead of myself. And ahead of that simple little worm, which for now is content to simply burrow in and enjoy summer. The timothy will go to seed soon enough.

BAD LUCK, GOOD LAUGHS

I had been traveling and living out of hotel rooms for the better part of a month and was looking forward to being a fake farmer for the afternoon. I say *fake* for a lot of reasons, including the fact that this will be the third summer my road schedule won't allow time for raising pigs (for now I raise *theoretical* pigs—a real streamliner chorewise, although the bacon runs a tad thin), my "crops" consist of two garden patches and a scattering of oats, and the tractor I was running is half a notch above lawn size and furthermore belongs to my mother-in-law.

Other than that, I am the real deal.

After greasing the rear-mounted tiller, I set out for the smaller garden patch. Over the years we've turned it into fair soil, in part by the annual addition of leaf compost. Using scraps of garden fencing, I built two small hoops to contain the leaves. I was reminded of this fact when I was backing the tiller into place and heard a snaky-screechy sound, which in fact turned out to be the wire hoops being sucked into the whirling tiller teeth.

How a guy fails to spot two wire hoops in a barren garden is a discussion I am not interested in having right now. Right there in the moment I was busy breathing deeply the country air and doing my best to exhale stress rather than swears or spit. In short, I was one red-faced yogi. Disengaging the power takeoff, I drove to the pole barn and fetched the wire nippers.

In fact, things went better than expected. The small-gauge wire snipped away easily, and in ten minutes I was back in the saddle. I finished the small plot and moved to the oat patch.

After harvesting the oats last fall, we ran chickens on this field, moving them from spot to spot with a portable fencing system that is part store-bought and part my own invention (my part consists of five-foot posts made of three-eighths-inch steel rebar with a custom ninety-degree-angle handle that allows them to be easily pushed into the earth). As I made my first pass with the tiller, it was nice to think of all that natural chicken enrichment spinning into the topsoil.

This time there was no screeching. The sound was more thunderous and car-crashy, similar I suppose to the sound of twin fifty-five-gallon oil drums being attacked with riot batons by angry heavy metal gods on speed.

I nearly dislocated my hip, I stomped the clutch so fast.

Of all the three-eighths-inch rebar posts we used last fall, I remembered to pick up all but two of them, which puts me somewhere around a 92 percent success rate, an "A" in anybody's book. But when I knelt down and lifted the shield on that tiller and saw the two overlooked posts wrapped around the shaft of that tiller tighter than a codependent anaconda, it definitely felt like an "F."

I shall count it an eternal blessing that neither my wife nor my children were home to hear the lamentations that then arose, although I cannot speak for the farmer in the valley below, and indeed his beef cows may still be wide-eyed.

But here's the thing: Within five minutes I had cooled down and was grinning, because I knew this setback was going to make a handful of people very happy. I require a lot of tricks to get through this life, and one I'm most grateful for is the working-class knucklehead fatalism so many of us grew up with wherein the worse your luck (excluding fatalities) the better the story— and the greater the delight of those on your wavelength. In other words, my brothers were gonna love this.

There is no removing three-eighths-inch rebar with "nippers" or even—as I quickly discovered—a hacksaw and bolt cutters, so I called my neighbor Denny, who lives right down the hill and has a cutting torch. When he asked what the problem was, I told him I'd let him see for himself but that it involved a power tiller and two five-foot pieces of rebar. The way he giggled made me think he'd probably enjoy meeting my brothers. Indeed, when I parked outside his shop and he lifted the shield and laid eyes on the astounding ferrous snarl, his face lit up and he said "Ho-HO! That's a GOOD one!"

The cutting torch made quick work of the mess, and the rest of that patch is tilled now. Made it through snarl-free. On Sunday evening our family got together as we often do. Nothing amps up your bad-luck story like tangible evidence of tragedy, so naturally I had taken several before and after photos. As my brothers passed the cellphone around and everyone haw-hawed at my ineptitude I couldn't have been happier.

And Denny definitely gets an invite to the next family reunion.

TRIMMING TREES

The trees lining both sides of our driveway have so encroached that their limbs interlock overhead. During the leafy seasons, it is calming to drive beneath the canopy, uplifting to see the bright spots of sun lasering through here and there. It is so lovely, in fact, that one hardly notices the weed-begotten potholes until the front tires drop into the hubs.

As the potholes reveal, I'm a big fan of entropy. Of letting things be so they can grow and decay in their own good time and in their own good way. It is pleasant to look at a neatly manicured lawn, or a well-weeded garden, or a smooth stretch of fresh black-top, but all in all (and less romantically, what we might be talking here is nothing but glorified procrastination, skewed priorities, and a dollop of sloth) we spend so much time knocking nature into line that sometimes it's nice to just let it be.

However, when the arrival of the UPS truck is announced by the sound of branches squealing against the side panels and thwacking the side mirrors, one is compelled to weigh beauty against utility. One is also reminded (with chimney fire season in the offing) that several of the fire trucks parked in the hall down the road require far greater clearance than a delivery van. Plus they are making ambulances bigger these days. And so it is that we have lately been trimming back the trees.

As with all projects, I had been working on this one in my mind for approximately three years and in fact had filed it under COMPLETE with an asterisk. So it was a disappointment that first evening when I strode out with my chainsaw and faced the reality of the logging to come. When my wife gently suggested that the project might move more quickly if we coordinated with the adjacent landowner (my mother-in-law, in fact) and scheduled a few family workdays where we'd all pitch in at once, I went through my usual petulant/dismissive stage (having nothing to do with my mother-in-law, but everything to do with my ingrained bullheaded stubbornness), then finally grudgingly agreed.

Naturally things are going at fivefold speed and efficiency. Not only is the driveway opening up, but we now have an unheard-of head start on next year's firewood (the making of firewood is another of my "mind-projects," and I am always disappointed in the universe when I go to the woodshed and find that all the splitting and stacking I visualized while sitting at my desk has once again failed to manifest in burnable form). At our current pace, another two or three sessions and the driveway should be accessible for another ten years.

As with any fresh haircut, the new look takes some getting used to, but over the winter entropy will regroup, and when the new leaves unfurl come spring, it will immediately commence recovering any ground lost.

Next: Fix the potholes? I dunno. Now and then, despite the spray-painted and bullet-riddled PIRVATE DRIVE sign I screwed to a popple tree (the typo is intentional—I intend that the sign deliver its message on a number of levels), strangers sneak up our drive for a look around. Last month two gentlemen in one of those very low-slung road-hugging hot rods showed up uninvited. I heard their stereo thudding five minutes before they arrived. I didn't show myself, but once they turned around in our yard to depart, I followed them in our old pickup to be sure they made it safely off the property. It took a while, because even driving three miles an hour (I clocked it) the understructure of their car continually scraped and ground against the busted-up blacktop. It sounded like a slow-motion avalanche at the tympani factory. It was an unexpected delight, so I figure entropy has earned the right to those potholes for at least one more year.

MOWER MAINTENANCE

I am not your leading lawn guy. Don't get me wrong—I admire a neat lawn, in very much the same way I admire a nicely knotted tie. Looks good, good for you for doing it, and I'll be over here in my ratty old T-shirt.

I figure as long as you can track the younger child's head above the clumps of orchard grass as she goes out to fetch the eggs, why burn excess time and gasoline in the name of aesthetics? This has less to do with any pretensions to efficiency and environmentalism than with a general apathy toward greensward. It may also track back to my childhood on the farm, when the point of cutting grass was to convert it into hay bales.

Among the benefits of living on a dead-end back forty farm—as we do now—I count the fact that no one ever drives by to look at the lawn. Which is a good thing, because our main mower is a real turf-bludgeoning beauty. It's an off-brand rider that came with the place. The deck rides at a slight angle, which leaves the lawn with a serrated look (frankly, with proper marketing and a GPS app I believe this could be pitched as a desirable contouring feature). It is also missing the entire hood. In that way it makes me sentimental for several of the cars I drove in the 1980s, most of which I bought from underneath a homemade FOR SALE sign and none of which ever rang the till at anything more than the low three figures.

I have always viewed riding lawn mowers as contributing to anemia of character, so when we moved here I insisted we purchase a push model so that the children might develop strong calves and morals. Six years later we occasionally use it to trim around the house or mulch some leaves, but mostly it collects dust in a corner back behind the rider, which—despite its dilapidated state—can do the job in a third of the time, and on this point I am in wholehearted agreement with my brother Jed, whom I have elsewhere and previously quoted as saying, "Mowin' the lawn is a *timed* event."

The grass was even taller than usual by the time I mowed for the first time this year. My excuse was based on the fact that I am a real stickler for regular lawn mower maintenance. I never let the machine go more than three—maybe five—years before I change the oil, and this was the year. I resolved not to spin a blade until it was done. And so when I finally got around to it the lawn resembled a crabgrass and dandelion preserve. But that faithful old wreck of a mower chewed through it, spitting out random silage clots all along the way.

Now it's time to mow again. Perhaps the grass has grown prohibitively high. I don't know, because I am on book tour and can't see it from here. A couple of weeks ago I looked at new mowers. I was eyeing the ones with the blower/bagger attachment, which would mean if we waited too long to mow at least we wouldn't have to jump over the windrows in order to set up the volleyball net. But then I saw the price tag and couldn't pull the trigger. Besides, I have another attachment for our old mower that's been working out real good, even when I'm gone. She's fifteen, and saving for college.

ZERK

If nothing else, my daughter can now identify a zerk.

I've been using the term for years, but until I sat down to write this piece and performed the obligatory Google, I hadn't realized it was derived from a proper name, that of Oscar U. Zerk, who was granted a patent for the lowercase zerk in 1929.

Zerks were a big part of my life in the early years, when my dad the farmer said the old-timers taught him that the two best ways to maintain machinery were to store it under a roof and make sure it got plenty of grease. When he sent me out to cut hay I knew he was actually sending me out to grease the haybine and *then* cut hay. When I worked on a hay crew in Wyoming, I always began my day crawling over, under, and around my swather, grease gun and rag in hand, hunting zerks. The day you found them all without referring to the manual you knew you were in for the long haul.

The zerk is a fitting designed to allow the insertion of grease into a bearing—if you're not familiar, in the most basic terms we're talking about any joint in a machine that rotates or flexes. Since the first time I heard it, "zerk" has always been one of my favorite words. It's fun to pronounce, for one thing. Satisfyingly abrupt and workmanlike, and yet, that entertaining *z* for fun. It's also the kind of word a typist with soft hands likes to carry in his back pocket for those conversational moments down at the fire hall when he wishes to imply knowledge more situationally substantive than the keyboard shortcut for a happy face emoji.

No matter how soft my hands, if I casually drop the term "zerk," I feel like I have calluses.

Like most parents, I'm never sure if I'm executing my responsibilities in a manner bound to produce a functional adult. We can only respond by teaching at every opportunity. And so it was I spent part of today teaching my teenaged daughter how to attach and detach the brush hog to and from the tractor before sending her out to buzz down an overgrown patch of pasture.

But first, I introduced her to the zerk. After giving her the speech about preserving machinery through application of grease and a roof (while thinking fondly of my father and the old-timers who taught him), I showed her how to run the grease gun, and then we made our way around the machine until it was well lubricated and ready to go.

There is so much we must teach our children. Lately I feel like I have been falling short. Not for lack of trying, mind you. It's just that the older they grow, the faster it goes, until you realize you're never going to cover everything, let alone make it stick. I don't know how I'm doing. Won't know, for a long time. But if my elder daughter ever owns her own brush hog, I have reason to believe she will provide it shelter and grease.

We are just now moving into that time when young men are beginning to make their way up our driveway in hope of making social calls on this same daughter. In order to thin the herd, there will have to be some sort of selection process. So far all of my suggestions have been rejected as draconian (Exactly!). But perhaps one day if she's looking into some fellow's eyes and the vote hangs at 50/50, she can ask him, "So, what's a *zerk*?"

Provide the correct answer, son, and you will have at the least earned further consideration.

"OKAY"

Late this summer my wife and I found ourselves engaged in a procedural disagreement involving a woodstove. Specifically, she wanted to proceed in one direction, and I wanted to proceed in another.

First she laid out her case. Then I laid out mine. When I finished, she smiled and said, "Okay."

I'm not sure how long a guy needs to be married before he figures out what "okay" really means. Apparently more than ten years, which is how long my wife has been using the word (usually accompanied by a slight elevation of the eyebrows) as a means of allowing me to follow the path of self-discovery—in particular, discovering that I am wrong.

Over this past wedded decade, I've had plenty of opportunities to identify the pattern: There was the time I gave her a polite instructional (some call it "mansplaining") on how the wiring on the cattle waterer worked; the time I dismissed the idea that we had to schedule the butcher three months ahead of time; the time I assured her that we had more than enough firewood to last the winter. Then there was the time during a blizzard when she asked if I might want to pre-plow in light of all the accumulation. Nah, I said, it'll just fill in right behind me . . . waste of time, gas, and effort . . . I'll get it in the morning . . . huff and puff. In each and every case there came a moment when I realized: Not only was I wrong, I was *demonstrably* (and sometimes *ridiculously*) wrong. In the case of the blizzard, I had failed to take into consideration an overnight temperature drop from near freezing to subzero—the result being that all access was locked in a solid block of concrete meringue against which the snowplow was powerless. I spent the day pecking away with the tractor loader, one bucket at a time, all the while nursing my ego and rehearsing my retraction.

More recently, I told my wife I needed to buy a trailer for book and band tours, as our diesel station wagon no longer holds all the merch and literature I've generated (to say nothing of my musical equipment creep, an affliction all players will recognize). "How about if you take the old van?" she asked, after which I provided a frowning recitation of all the reasons this was not a workable option, beginning with comparative gas mileage and concluding with general minivan disdain (but not referencing the station wagon's heated seats). "Okay," she said. Then an unexpected mechanical issue with the car forced me to take the van on the first leg of the tour. When I swung by the house a week later, my wife asked if I wanted help moving everything back over to the station wagon now that it was fixed. Oh, no need for all that extra work, I said, manfully, I'll stick with the van for now. I did not admit that I had discovered how much easier it was to load and unload the van day after day as opposed to crouching under the hatchback of that station wagon.

"Okay," she said. This time the word carried a little different meaning, but I'd say we were still operating within range of the central theme.

Last year our old woodstove developed a crack in the firebox. In preparation for replacing it, my wife and I went to several vendors, did online research, and talked to friends. As always, this approach left me deeply informed and pretty much paralyzed. So the day we finally found a stove that met all of our criteria, I suggested we buy it right then and there, and have it delivered, as I was leaving for book tour the next day. "But I think we might be able to do a better deal . . . ," said my wife, and I admit to some impatience when I replied with a recitation of all the time and energy we'd already expended, and that what we really needed to do was buy this stove and move on.

You already know what she said.

That was two months ago. I'm finally back home from book tour, and last night as I stoked the new woodstove I admired how much more efficient it was, and how much larger the firebox was, and the high quality of the materials and construction, and how it retailed far beyond our budget . . . or would have, except that after I left on tour, my wife (in the company of my mother-in-law) went to one more store and cut a deal on a high-end floor model that wound up saving us more money than I spent on gas for the entire tour.

Okay.

Our old farmhouse is really showing its age. Lately my wife has been reading books about the micro home movement. I told her it simply won't work for us.

I expect I'll be living in a shoebox within the month.

CAT-A-FRAT

The last of the gashes has nearly healed, visible only as a thin red thread running half the length of my left forearm. My relationship with the cat who did the carving has healed as well, although I can't blame the cat if it retains some reservations regarding my character for the duration.

Our family returned home after dark. Halfway up the hill, a pair of tongue-lolling dogs came panting into our headlights. I recognized them as belonging to a neighbor two miles distant. We'd kenneled them previously, so I thought it best we do so again and give him a call in the morning. The dogs were damp and we caught a whiff of skunk. Not wanting them in the van, my elder daughter offered to walk them up our driveway (it is also possible she spotted an opportunity for unsupervised texting, but let us not be picayune).

At the garage, our three cats—who normally greet us there—were absent. Our younger daughter, a self-described "cat lady" who breaks into tears at the mere mention of Previous Cats Since Passed, emitted a worry noise. I stepped out and called and soon two kitties came. They were skittish and kept looking over their shoulders. It occurred to me that perhaps the dogs had been up here already.

The dog kennel (put up by a previous owner—we do not have a dog) is attached to a small pump house that serves as a kitty condo. Depositing the two cats safely within, I latched the door and set out to find the third cat. In the meantime, elder daughter arrived with the dogs and secured them in the kennel. Just then I located the third cat, huddled behind the garage.

My suspicions that the visiting dogs had been harassing the home team felines were confirmed when I got within thirty feet of the kennel and the hair along that cat's spine flared up in a furry ridge. Picking it up and holding it to my chest, I petted it and made reassuring noises. Out of fear that it would run off into the night never to be seen again, triggering fresh cat-lady despair, I was completely focused on depositing it safely in the cat condo— despite the fact that we had to pass through the kennel to do so. In retrospect, I was not thinking clearly, but in my defense it was late and I was motivated by the love of a child. And so it was, as I reached for the kennel gate and the dogs woofed and the cat struggled to leap free, I only tightened my grip, obsessed by the idea of the feline disappearing forever and all the tears to follow. In a trice the cat clawed me from wrist to elbow, bit me twice and deeply in both hands, and only then did I let go to stand there bleeding like a Wes Craven extra as the animal vanished into the darkness.

There followed quite a rodeo. At its conclusion, the dogs were transferred to the garage, my elder daughter wheedled the final cat back to safety, and I retired to the house to bathe in hydrogen peroxide while Googling "cat bites," which returns some bracing info. By the following midmorning the dogs were reunited with their owner, and by noon the cat that cut me was back on purring terms and sleeping in my office chair. Now, three weeks out, I am infection-free and nearly healed.

I wish there was some sort of moral to the story beyond *don't be me,* although this is the point at which readers tend to *provide* me with moral guidance, because A) cats, and B) what were you *thinking?* I shall await all correspondence (it can't be worse than a frantic armful of claws and teeth) and can for now only shake my head in wonder while preemptively responding in the schoolyard jargon of my cat-happy eight-year-old: *I know, right?*

TIME TO READ

It's time to read the book.

I don't know which book. It could be one of the many lining the bookshelves surrounding my daughter's bed. It could be one of the many tiling her bedroom floor. It could be one she brought home from school on Wednesday, which is her favorite school day because it is library day. It could be one we've read fifty-seven times already because it has that one part where the frog's face turns "more red than green," and boy, that line never gets old.

It's time to read the book, because my daughter has come to me, teeth brushed and pajamas on, with several selections tucked beneath one arm. She can read those books on her own now, but still asks to be read to every night, and we oblige, because, well, *literacy*, sure, and because like so many parents we've absorbed the stats linking reading and any number of academic achievements and life skills, but of course as any parent knows, mostly we read to her as a form of spiritual investment and reinvestment. *In*vestment because we hope she will carry the memories of this bedtime ritual with her throughout her life, and *re*investment because every time I cradle her on my lap or squeeze in beside her on the couch and open the book I am collecting interest on my own fond memories of my parents doing the same. The memories of my mother and father reading to me are precious not just because they introduced me to words and stories but because the words and stories came with a subliminal message: You are important to me, so important that I will pause what I am doing here in grown-up world so that *my* time can become *our* time.

Speaking of pausing, let me do that and reframe, lest I autocast myself as uber-sensitive father of the year. In truth, many is the night I'll look for a reason to cut the session short, or lobby for the slimmest tome in the stack because there is still work to be done or I'm flat-out ready for bed myself. For all the inherent joys of cuddling in and reading with your child, it can also have a profound narcoleptic effect. (Thus the counterintuitive upside of thick "chapter" books—with no expectation of finishing, you can always rouse just long enough to say, "This is a good place to stop," and then stagger off to your own bed.) Finally, it is incumbent upon me to admit that for a number of reasons ranging from distant obligations to general work schedules my wife reads to the youngster more frequently than I. And as long as I'm admitting things, I will reveal that last week the tot said, "Mom reads longer than you do," and I have no reason to suspect this is not so.

But now it's time to read the book. She's up there waiting with it, so I'll climb the stairs and make my way through the scattered dolls and dress-up clothes and probably some dirty socks, and I'll sit on the edge of the bed and we'll adjust the Crayola lamp just right and I'll do the voices and put rhythm in the rhymes if it's that kind of book, and tired or not I will cherish the way the child settles in for the story, enchanted into stillness by language, drawn close at the close of day, drawn close—I pray—for a time far beyond this.

It's time to read the book.

ROAD

ROLLING ALONG

If time and life keep on track—an assumption no mortal must make, unless that mortal is required to produce a newspaper column eleven days before it is published—by the time this hits print, I will be midway through book tour, having returned from forays into Minnesota and Ohio in order to peddle my typing right here in my home state before dropping down to Illinois and back over to Iowa. As a road dog of long standing (having been raised in part by truckers and country music roadies), I don't mind racking up the miles, although as a father and husband I do find that the old horse tends to gaze over his shoulder toward the barn more often than he used to.

Book tour is a privilege. I tool around from town to town, stopping here and there to talk about stories and writing, and best of all, I get to meet readers and say thank you right to their faces. You never know, while poking away at the keyboard (and no key of mine is more worn than *backspace/delete*) all alone in the wee hours, whether or not anyone will read what you produce, and furthermore whether they'll make it all the way to the end, and finally, whether they'll cherish or regret the time sacrificed in the effort. (Of course some take the time to post their assessments in this regard on the World Wide Web so that I am not left to wonder.) But you hope you will connect here and there, and book tour allows that to happen in person. Readers have changed my life, and they also help me make the house payment: I do my best to write with that thought ever close at hand.

Some readers come bearing gifts, which are neither required nor expected but are certainly welcome, and sometimes surprising. On the first stop of this tour a man commented on the length and breadth of my itinerary, said he wanted to make sure I had enough to eat, and handed me a shopping bag filled to overflowing with Wisconsin-based jerked meat products. We're talking *poundage.* I don't know what sort of literary presents Lorrie Moore or Salman Rushdie receive, but for a guy spending four weeks driving around Wisconsin, jerky is perfect, plus I saw some cheese sticks in there.

Over the years the gifts I have been given on book tour include my very first farm-fresh green eggs (now we raise our own, inspired in part by that gift), tomato plants, snickerdoodles, fire department patches, vintage fire extinguishers, a MIND THE GAP sign from the London Underground (but given to me in honor of the gap between my front teeth), mirrors for my 1951 International pickup, a carburetor for my 1951 International pickup, a vintage plumb-bob (a reference to an obscure passage in one of my books), a note offering to answer any septic tank questions I might ever have, a hand-crafted and ornately decorated miniature two-holer outhouse (with its own carrying case), and once, a box of live 30–06 cartridges.

There is an old trucking song made popular by Del Reeves called "Looking at the World through a Windshield." That's pretty much how book tour unrolls (although Del sings about Daddy sending *all of his love from 'Frisco Bay,* and rolling *down around Dallas,* whereas for me it's more like sending all of my love from Des Moines and rollin' through Dallas up there in Barron County). I am an entourage of one—chauffeur, roadie, head of security— driving from town to town ready to tell stories, shake hands, say thanks, and keep going until the last hand is shook.

It's a pretty good deal. Until the jerky runs out.

DUCKING FAME

Once, for a split second in 2002, I thought I was famous. My ego first began to swell when I did a book signing in Nashville and more than thirty people showed up. *Yessir,* I thought to myself as I drove away from the bookstore that evening, *the Mike train is rolling.*

The next stop was Memphis. The publisher put me up in the Peabody Hotel, a swankish old place. Italianate marble doodads, pianist in the lobby, doormen in top hats, a fountain at the center of the grand lobby. Not my standard Motel 6 or Super 8 situation. Also, the Peabody has world-renowned ducks. The ducks live atop the hotel. Every morning, a uniformed attendant gathers the ducks from their rooftop lodgings and escorts them to the elevator bank, where they enter the center elevator and descend to the lobby. When the doors open, they waddle up a red carpet and into the marble fountain for a swim. The ducks keep a punctual schedule and the carpet is always lined with tourists and hotel guests who turn out to witness the historic procession.

It was a three-and-a-half-hour drive from Nashville and I got to the Peabody well after midnight. Before I turned in, I set my alarm for five a.m. for the first in a series of telephone radio interviews. It seemed like my head hardly hit the pillow before I was live on the air, pretending to be awake. But hey: such is the price of fame.

By the time the interviews were over and checkout time arrived I'd had about four hours of sleep and looked like it. Stuffing my clothes into my roller bag and slinging my backpack over one shoulder, I left my room and punched up the first available downbound elevator.

I was asleep on my feet when the elevator doors opened to a storm of flashbulbs. My eyes snapped wide open and all I could see was a red carpet stretching before me and flanked by a sea of people, many of them squinting at me through viewfinders. There I was, framed in the elevator door, unshaven, baggy-eyed, and toting my own luggage. The comic image was heightened by the fact that in those days I had long hair and dressed like I was raised by a wandering pack of country music roadies.

But all these people! So wild to see me! Just as I had my first coherent thought—*Oprah must have picked my book!*—the flashbulbs stopped and the titters began. Then the lobby filled with laughter, and I realized: In my fog, I had managed to intercept the elevator intended to collect the dang ducks. I tried to zip out of the way, but the little wheels on my suitcase got hung up in the carpet, and I had to scuttle around for a while until I got everything untangled and smoothed out. By the time I escaped, I was as red as that rug.

That evening I arrived at the bookstore fifteen minutes early. Chairs had been set up near a fireplace and seven people were already seated. *Seven people and still fifteen minutes to go,* I thought. *We'll hit double figures, easy. Not bad for an unknown cheesehead in Memphis. All aboard the Mike train.* Just then the manager got on the P.A. "Ladies and gentlemen," she said, "author Michael Perry will be here this evening to discuss his latest book—if you'd like to meet Mr. Perry, please join us in the chairs over by the fireplace."

At which point, all seven people looked at each other in alarm, then split.

No one ever did show up.

Since then, things have gone fine. I make a living, but I don't need a security detail to go to Farm & Fleet. And now when I go to Memphis I stay in the Super 8 where I belong. But I like to think that now and then somewhere in this nation—shoot, possibly even in other parts of the world—someone will be sorting through a forgotten set of photographs or videos from that time they went to Memphis, and there I will be, a startled goofball in baggy shorts and scuffed boots, bound for a book signing where no one showed up, but for just that one split second at least as famous as a couple of ducks.

MODEL BEHAVIOR

Shortly after I stepped into the elevator, I was surrounded by supermodels. As we ascended to the fifteenth floor it occurred to me that I was probably the only person present who had begun the day by chipping frozen poultry manure out of the door jamb of a chicken coop.

I had flown into LaGuardia Airport two hours earlier, stale from the standard all-day flight delays and a two-hour creep-and-crawl taxi ride across the Brooklyn Bridge into Manhattan. I was traveling under the credit card and graces of someone classier than I and had been put up in a boutique hotel in Soho. The lobby air was infused with the scent of bamboo and citrus; the waiting area was appointed with strategically stacked and tattered suitcases, antique glassware, and people in artfully knotted scarves. I was happy to be there, and thank you. There is the temptation to be all hickety-shucks about stuff, but unrelenting mockery is its own form of condescension even when directed toward an impeccably staged wingback chair.

That said, I was not prepared for all the supermodels. Later I would learn I had arrived at the peak influx days leading up to Fashion Week (which somehow had not made it onto my calendar), but for the moment I stood stock-still on that tiny elevator, a flat-footed toad among herons, immobilized not so much by fear of attack but from a fear of dirtying up the air. I had this troubling mental image of my fashion aura flaking off to drift through the citrus diffusions like low-class floaty dandruff, the models breaking into uncontrolled spasms of career-derailing puffy-eyed sneezing fits triggered by airborne allergens redolent of Farm & Fleet (pants, T-shirt, flannel shirt), Fruit of the Loom (gray tube socks), and the late Ralph's Boot & Shoe (clodhoppers, possibly infused with trace elements of chicken poop). My undies were designer brand—Tommy Hilfiger—but only because that's what was in the bin the day my wife broke a twenty at Savers.

From Barbie dolls to soap ads, popular culture is slowly moving toward the idea that there are many ways to be beautiful, but the models on the elevator were all from the classic mode—each far taller than I and one-third my circumference. In fact, the only person approaching my dimensions was a stern-browed woman who herded the models aboard by barking in French while pecking at her smartphone like a vulture tying to stab the last of the rib meat off a deer carcass. It was not impossible to imagine her lining them up at feeding time, doling out a lettuce leaf and half a cigarette. When I exited the elevator at the eleventh floor I believe everyone involved felt some relief.

Once inside my room I went to the window and pulled open the drapes, so I could observe the universe of illuminated windows, each one a reminder that I was in the presence of millions of lives unfolding in real time. I love doing this in big cities. I find it especially helpful during those self-centered stretches when I have convinced myself I am not only shouldering the world, but serving as its axis. I am reminded that there are an infinity of paths through this life, and I'm lucky to be on mine.

There are moments—on that elevator, for instance—when I wish I was leaner, or shinier, or smoother. More *haute,* couture or otherwise. That I might so immaculately drape and knot a scarf as to create the illusion of louche disregard. Instead I am now back home slouched in a half-busted recliner with my cheap socks extended toward the woodstove, clad in a Packers hoodie as I scratch out the last lines of this column. Night has fallen, my chickens are secure in their coop, ours is the only lit window visible for a mile, and somewhere the supermodels are supermodeling, as supermodels ought to do.

UP IN THE AIR

Up here the sun has already dropped below the distant edge of a horizon formed by a broad plain of furrowed clouds. The western sky is anemic pink and draining to pale blue. After a series of flight cancellations and delays that nowadays seem so commonplace it would be easier on everyone involved if boarding passes were printed in erasable ink, we—a scatter of unacquainted passengers on a half-filled cigar tube of a jet—have departed the Dane County airport and are airborne for the quick hop to Chicago.

Just prior to boarding, I spoke with my daughters by phone. It was good to hear their voices. I am in the middle of a month-long book tour, and have seen them only once—and then for only a matter of hours—since the tour commenced. I am thus predisposed to feeling maudlin, and now, looking out into the darkening sky with no earth in sight, I imagine them hundreds of miles away and tens of thousands of feet below at the kitchen table in our old farmhouse with warm yellow light spilling from the windows into the darkness all around. In mentally triangulating from that image to my current position in seat 12A, I render myself melancholy. To counter this self-centered slide, I summon the image of friends and family who work in the trucking industry or serve in the military; comparatively speaking my journey is but a merry side trip, and I try never to forget it.

At O'Hare, I am hoping for a connecting flight to Columbus, Ohio, where I am taking one day away from book tour in order to speak with a group of hospice volunteers. I use the word "hoping" in light of the day's accumulated airline hiccups, which began when my original flight was canceled sixteen hours before it was due to take off. And indeed, when we land in Chicago, I am greeted by a text message alerting me to a gate change. Before I make it up the jetway, the phone pings again: a second gate change. Then, a third text message: the flight has been delayed.

Half an hour later, the flight is delayed again.

Then comes another gate change.

By now those of us on the delayed flight are beginning to recognize each other as we migrate from gate to gate. No one seems especially cranky; rather, we troop along with an air of resigned camaraderie. It is getting late now. An hour previous the gate lounges were filled to overflowing; now there are empty seats all around. The concourse is as hushed as a funeral parlor, the occasional noise deadened by the carpet.

Again, the phone pings. Another delay.

The Starbucks barista kills the lights and draws a curtain around the coffee kiosk—now we are truly alone.

Another ping. At this point, no one is even reacting. We are all reading or texting or staring at screens. An alarm sounds and blares for five minutes. Everybody looks, nobody moves. Including me. When it finally goes silent, I think: *we are sitting ducks.*

At midnight, we are still waiting. A departing gate agent has left a microphone keyed open. It issues a steady rustle of static through the speakers. At first it is irritating. Fifteen minutes later, it sounds like soft rain falling on a tin roof.

Finally we are in the air. The flight is rough. On the descent to Columbus raindrops flash like bullets in the strobes. The plane is dropping and bucking and kicking sideways. We land with a bounce and a lurch. In a few hours I will be gathering with a roomful of people who make it their duty to ease the living gently into dying. *Everything need not be a parable, Spanky,* I think to myself as I wait for sleep. *Sometimes it is enough to simply ride out the delays, and be happy where you are.*

COUNTRY BOY IN THE CITY

Last Sunday I thought of Anthony Shadid.

It was morning. The day's first coffee was at hand. Rather than my usual view of the back forty, I was at a window overlooking a city center. Outside the sun was blessedly bright, the air was shorts-and-T-shirt warm, and along the sidewalks ranks of tulips bloomed. We were weeks past the first day of spring, but this was the first day that *felt* like the first day of spring.

Just beyond my vantage point, a wedge-shaped intersection was under repair, the crosswalks replaced by temporary rubber mats laid over uneven gravel. A young couple came to the point of the wedge and stopped. Raising his free hand, the man pointed right. Raising hers, the woman pointed left. They unclasped their joined hands and started off in separate directions. Then, after stopping to shake her head, the woman relented and rejoined the man. Shortly afterward a very elderly couple appeared at the same intersection. They too were holding hands, and they too were shaking their heads and pointing in opposite directions. In fact, they both leaned away from each other, pulling apart but never letting go their grasp. Finally they chose one direction and took it. Soon came a third couple. They stopped at the same point, argued vigorously and angrily over left versus right, then, unable to agree, spun and turned back in the direction from which they had come.

It struck me that this intersection would be of great interest to sociologists (or at the very least, Dr. Phil), but mostly I dispensed with assumptions and interpretation and simply enjoyed the human movie. A little boy posed beaming in the bucket of an idled skid steer holding a toy version of the exact same machine while his father snapped a phone photo. The young woman mounting a bike bearing a sticker that said, YOU'D LOOK HOTTER IN A HELMET and pedaling vigorously away—without a helmet. One man stopping another to point out some element of architecture on the roofline overhead. A tot perched on his grandfather's shoulders, bobbing along above all the grown-ups. A youth carrying a clear plastic cone filled with flowers. A man standing alone beside a streetlight, talking on a phone while swiveling his head back and forth, clearly trying to locate the other person on the line. A couple walking a harlequin Great Dane the size of an abbreviated Holstein. A woman exiting a bakery with a muffin in a paper bag, stopping as she recognized a friend, then eating the muffin, piece by broken-off piece, as the two chatted until the muffin was gone and they parted.

Taken as a whole, the scene outside my window was busy, but not hectic. In general, people were *ambling*. You don't get a lot of *ambling* anymore. You'd think country folk would amble, but mostly we blow past each other at the speed of internal combustion. I am country by chance, choice, and predilection, but mornings like this are why I enjoy my big-city visits. There is a vibrancy—a human energy—that invigorates me but also provides a useful corrective to my own creeping reverse provincialism. For all talk of putative rural neighborliness, in the big city you have to actually get along with strangers on a daily basis to make the whole thing work. Whether you're sharing the subway or the sidewalk, you tacitly agree to come out and cooperate. There's no holing up at the terminus of a dead-end drive to cultivate self-perceived self-reliance between trips to town for supplies.

I was considering this and the handful of sidewalk cafes open for business in the sunny new day when journalist Anthony Shadid came to mind. In short, he was a man who devoted his

abbreviated life to telling the stories of common people struggling for normalcy amongst the worst human strife. I met Anthony only once, but during our one quiet conversation he said
that of all the casualties of war, few were more costly than the
small moments ("gentle simply by virtue of their being ordinary,"
he once wrote) of civility: the open-air stroll, the impromptu sidewalk conversation, the peace agreements inherent in strangers
having coffee elbow-to-elbow.

In the midst of the torn-up intersection, the construction company had planted a porta-potty. It stood right there in plain view,
a temporary monument to the idea that whichever direction we
point, we are all organic humans in the same boat, so why all the
fighting? Anthony Shadid would have put it more eloquently, but
when I stepped out into the sunlight later, it was thanks to him
that I felt all the more deeply my gratitude for this simple sunny
morning, a country boy content in the city.

ROAD TRIP

Here in the fambulance (some say minivan) we are headed west, en route to rendezvous with friends and family in Nebraska, Wyoming, and Colorado.

My wife is driving as I type. (If grant money is available, there is a boutique motion sickness research project begging to be done in that I am utterly unable to read in the car—one paragraph and I'm bound to barf—and yet I can stare at my laptop screen while typing from here to the Rockies and not be bothered.) Our daughters are strapped in behind us, listening to an audiobook and drawing in sketchpads. For purposes of entertainment in transit, there will be games of license plate bingo and "I Spy," and we will allow some sessions with the portable DVD player (our van is of a vintage predating—or a model precluding—preinstalled screens) for a movie or two after dark, but there will also be extended (some say *enforced*) stretches of frank boredom (and very possibly sulking) (the kids too), which my wife and I suspect reinforces the ability to think for oneself.

I will try to make it all the way to the Minnesota border before uttering my first "in my day" declaration regarding the Spartan conditions of travel *in my day*, which in my retelling were just short of Conestoga. In fact, there was a stretch during my childhood in which our large family's transportation was reduced to one old farm truck, and half the clan rode to church in the back, wrapped in sleeping bags and protected from the wind (but not the feed dust) by a sheet of plywood Dad bolted over the bed. On my first true road trip—from Wisconsin to Wyoming—Dad let me drive I-80 at the age of sixteen while he napped on a mattress in the back of the van, an act of abiding trust and foolish faith that astounds me still. Perhaps he was a closet fatalist. Regardless, much has changed in the era of shoulder belts and air bags.

Thus far in the trip there has been little in the way of sightseeing, although we have spotted several hundred immobile wind turbines, a World War II–era International Harvester fire truck being trailered to a new home, and a sign for a business purporting to serve "all your meat needs," which seems the heartiest sort of promise. Also, the grain silos keep getting bigger. Sadly, by the looks of much of the corn—uneven and stunted in the wake of all the early-season drenching—I wonder if they will be filled to capacity come fall.

It is inevitable, on a trip like this, that at some point the van will feel too small. The cycles of family harmony will slip in and out of sync. Fuel will run low on all fronts. But for the moment, the sense of adventure is still keen. The younger child has made less than fifty requests to watch a movie, and we are running a 50/50 ratio in the category of planned/unplanned bathroom stops. We're a fairly roadworthy crew, whether driving our domestic highways, hiking seaside trails in the Caribbean, or hitching a ride on a bus in Central America. Nothing dramatic, but we get around and get along. Best of all, we know that over time memory has a way of minimizing the moment of grumpiness in a South Dakota rest stop while simultaneously enhancing the glow of campfire and the scent of s'mores later that night.

Back home, the chickens have a babysitter, as does the homestead itself. It's good to know folks who'll keep an eye on things. To have neighbors who make it a point to be neighborly. Who make it so that when we are ready to go home, it will be good to go home.

But for now, we're westbound.

ON THE ROAD AGAIN

The other night our family slept in a tent in Murdo, South Dakota, where—after a day of absorbing blazing I-90 sun through the windshield—we were lulled to sleep by a cool breeze and the nonstop flatulent rattle of the nation's motorcycles accelerating down the on-ramp, headed for Sturgis. This is the second year in a row we have timed our westbound travels to coincide with the opening weekend of the massive piston-driven pilgrimage. One needs to up one's motorcycle awareness, which is fine in any case. It also provides the opportunity to conduct an offhand rolling anthropological study cross-referencing a range of class and cultural boundaries that include philosophy (to trailer or not to trailer), literature (I think here of two "found" texts that passed me on the left, each emblazoned across the back of a sleeveless T-shirt, and each unprintably incisive; while I can't say either author was bound to win fresh hearts and minds, I assigned full marks for pith and concision), and social status (you, sir, reflected in the chrome pipes and mirrored goggles passing by, are piloting a thirteen-year-old family van containing yogurt cups—please remain in the slow lane).

Our travels thus far have been blessedly uneventful in the sense that there have been no unexpected adventures beyond a child's brand-new flipflop lost at a rest stop somewhere between Minnesota and Wall Drug. There were tears, but nothing compared to the time we left her older sister's favorite fluffy pink velour piglet in a snowbound parking lot of a Nebraskan Super 8.

And so the long-term benefits of family travel accrue—despite the close quarters and occasional sharp words we not only spin new stories, we are given reason to revisit the older ones. This trip included a stop at Wounded Knee, which is another sort of story altogether. My hope is that through travel our children will gather their own stories but not in a way that will satisfy or lull them into failing to consider the stories of others. That does not mean they haven't been allowed a DVD or two along the way, or a peek at the Corn Palace. This is a family road trip, not a rolling PhD program. In fact, every one of us (from the age of eight to fifty) very much enjoyed our time at Carhenge. We also armed the young one with an erasable whiteboard and played many miles of analog hangman.

The Murdo campground had a pool, which is always a treat for the kids, although in this case, "had" became a relevant term, as prior to our arrival one of the pools had gone missing, its previous presence framed in a tumble of semicircular decking that created the appearance of a decrepit shipyard dock marooned in weeds. A second, smaller pool was still extant, although it looked as if it needed a good cleaning, which I assume will be more easily accomplished should the ownership ever decide to fill it with water. At the moment it is of little use for much more than a swim meet for mimes.

The price was right, however, and the showers were functional and clean. We woke to a fresh, sunny day. You get your basics, you are already living in the world of privilege. Drive on.

VISITING AN OLD BOSS

I was sixteen when I hired on with the Wyoming ranch. My boss was a redheaded man named Willie, with long arms, a bull chest, and strength enough to execute submission holds on two ranch hands simultaneously even if they did have the jump on him in the weeds after dark, as my friend Flip and I discovered one evening behind the cookhouse.

The first summer I worked for him, Willie was a newlywed, roaring off to Sunday meeting with his bride in a fat-tired four-wheel-drive pickup fitted with chrome side pipes. When I returned for the second summer, the fat tires had been replaced with skinny, and the chrome pipes were gone. The third summer, I spied a diaper on the dashboard. Now he is a grandfather, and I'm sneaking up on a half-century, a dad with daughters of my own.

We visited the ranch last week, and although our stay was brief, there was time to push the chairs back after dinner and retell the old stories. My daughters especially enjoyed the one about the time Willie and his wife, Kathy, took me with them on a trip to Rawlins for supplies. The pickup had been replaced by a Bronco by then. Willie was driving, I was riding shotgun, and Kathy was in the backseat with the couple's newborn son. Looking for a meal on the way home, we pulled into a fast-food drive-through and nearly collided with a man in a Monte Carlo. The position of our vehicles put us at roughly a forty-five-degree angle, and Mr. Monte Carlo was close enough that when he made an obscene gesture out his window and dropped what in contemporary times we call an "F-bomb," I could hear him clearly. In my politest churchgoing tones, I said, "Pardon me, sir?"

He repeated the singular oath.

"Sir, we have a woman and a child in this vehicle. I must ask you to refrain from such language." I was deploying Victorian politeness as a goad. I did this a lot in my youth, often while feeling quite pleased with myself.

Again, he repeated the same two-word phrase.

"My goodness, sir," I said, now adding a drop of condescension to the faux civility. "For such a large man, you have a terribly tiny vocabulary."

Boy, that did the trick. Mr. Monte Carlo flung open his door and came roaring out from behind the wheel, all the while inviting me to eschew banter for pugilism. In the process he confirmed before my very eyes that yes, he *was* a very large man. Conversely, he punched some holes in my previous verbal assessment in that he was now interspersing his favorite cuss word with foam-flecked selections of a wide-ranging and naughty order. I was reviewing my options and envisioning the amount of plaster we'd need to patch me up assuming I survived (it was a good time for envisioning, as my eyes were open really wide), when there came a tremendous metallic thunder on the order of someone deploying a rubber mallet against a tympani. It was Willie, who had exited the car, rounded the front bumper, and—as he headed straight for Mr. Monte Carlo—brought the flat of his hand down on the Bronco hood like an ape slapping a tire and bellowed, "BRING IT ON!"

The man leaped into his car and sped away.

I spent the next twenty minutes assuring Willie that I totally had his back on that one but when we got back home we'd better take the Bronco into the ranch shop and figure out what the heck was wrong with the door latch because for the life of me I hadn't been able to get it open or I would have totally thumped that dude.

A few years back Willie went a few rounds with cancer. Nowadays he needs some oxygen at night to fend off a slow-moving but terminally progressive lung condition. But he's far from housebound. The day we arrived he was out with the hay crew, and the day we left he was running a payloader. Most days he's working just like the old days, often beside his son—the one who filled that dashboard diaper all those years ago but is now running the ranch.

As the twice-and-thrice-told tales were resurrected around the ranch dinner table, I could see my daughters trying to form images of the two bald men before them as thirty years younger and able to wrassle around in the gravel without taking the next three days off for kinked necks and liniment. Perhaps they picked up on some subtext regarding the impermanence of life and the blessings of friendship, and how the first is eased by the latter. Probably they saw just two old guys rambling.

I do know they giggled at the idea of Dad getting himself into a jam with his yapper, and Willie bailing him out. Thirty years on, those giggles made the whole trip worth it, so Mr. Monte Carlo, if you're out there, listen up: Bless you.

HOME AGAIN

After a twelve-day family trip, we are safely home. It was a good journey and the ol' three-hubcapped fambulance held up well, taking us through the baking-hot South Dakota Badlands, up to Mt. Rushmore, deep into the Rockies, and finally back home to Wisconsin, where, thanks to our neighbors, the chickens were doing fine.

I can report that the Corn Palace in Mitchell, South Dakota, is undergoing a major makeover, in order, I suppose, to compete with more commercial attractions actually visible from the interstate. I cannot speak to the future of the Corn Palace, but my wife and I have done our part to introduce one more generation to its wonders. In fact, I have to say my children were more taken with it than I was at their age, perhaps because the idea of creating a massive art installation with cob corn seems all the more marvelous in the age of high-def television screens and NFL scoreboards the size of Rhode Island. We also paid a visit to the eighty-foot brontosaurus along I-90, another testament to the enduring thrall of giant concrete things even in this the digital age.

Based on the notes I've received from readers, I have come to believe that dragging our kids through seven states in two weeks will yield a few precious memories, but will also likely cause them to remember their parents as under-showered, map-obsessed road tramps who fed them lunch meat from a cooler within sniffing range of the dumpster out back of an Iowa rest stop. Then again it isn't always the postcard moments that resonate. During one juncture of this most recent trip we reminisced about favorite moments from previous trips, and my elder daughter said it was the subzero evening when we took the children into a truck stop in Des Moines way past their bedtimes and—in light of accumulated road wear and the miles ahead—allowed them to choose any treat they wished as long as it didn't come in a round tin imprinted with a surgeon general's warning. Despite all the plastic-wrapped sugar bombs available, our elder daughter chose one of those prepackaged dill pickles, an industrial-sized monster sealed within a plastic sleeve and its own juices. Go figure. She was still gnawing at it when we pulled into Eau Claire County, predawn.

As with most parents, we set up these trips with a subagenda. It is our hope that travel will instill in our children a love—and even more, an *appreciation*—of freedom. We hope when they look out the window across endless Wyoming grasslands, or order *pho* at a restaurant in Little Saigon just off Alameda Street in Denver, they will realize things are not the same everywhere, and that humanity blooms in infinite forms—when it is allowed to bloom. That sometimes if life is pulling you down, the best thing you can do is pull up stakes. That last phrase, of course, is a platitude depending on privilege: the privilege of being equipped and enabled to move freely and—within the bounds of common sense— without concern for one's safety. I don't know that we can—or should—construct a family trip around talking points, and it's not like I snuck a PowerPoint presentation into the portable DVD player, but I sure hope that somewhere in the substrata of our children's consciousness the memories of family travel will lead them to remember that nothing is to be taken for granted, that compassion is in order (as we will likely require plenty sent our way), and that we should never confuse our good fortune with just deserts.

That, and the fact that if you're looking for a treat to last for miles and a memory to last for years, you can do worse than a vacuum-sealed truck stop pickle.

SPRING COLOR TOUR

This past weekend, the portable portion of my self-employment led me to traverse the state from my home in rural Fall Creek (near Eau Claire) to Fish Creek (in northern Door County), then downstate on a diagonal to Richland Center, and finally back north to home.

Much of this extended commute was conducted in cold, gray weather interspersed with bouts of cold, gray rain. Excepting the evergreens (and even many of these appeared freezer-burned by the winter just passed), the earth's natural palette was limited to a narrow range of washed-out tans and anemic browns, with only the faintest wash of green here and there to imply more verdant days ahead.

When it comes to windshield-based tourism, only an obtuse crank would question why civic boosters tend to focus on autumn's glorious transformations by promoting Fall Color Tours, but if I was in charge (there are measures in place to prevent that, mainly, the perceptive voting public) I might focus more attention on this dead seasonal segment wedged between barren white winter and jungly green summer. Nothing to see during that stretch, you say? I submit there is even *more* to see. The earth is naked, and nothing is hidden. In fact, following on the spirit of the Fall Color Tour, I would designate this the Frank Assessment Tour, the tour where you really see what's out there.

Along the roadways the ditch grasses are pressed flat, so you can easily spot the thawed roadkill, the off-cast plastics, the odd bits of Styrofoam, the errant hubcaps, the beer cans, and the shredded tire peelings truckers refer to as "gators." Shopping bags snagged in the sumac, rotten lumber piles in backyard briars, that rusty rototiller behind the yard barn, everything is right out in the open.

Entropy itself is on display: the old shed tilting another three degrees, the barn with the bowed roof that finally gave in under record snows and fell flat, the abandoned hay rake with its steel wheels a quarter-inch deeper into the topsoil—over winter they are draped in snow, the sharp lines softened; in summer they are cloaked in shade and wild cucumber. In this the week (or so) of preawakening, they sit stranded right out in the open.

That is not to say this is a time without beauty. I especially enjoy the chance to peek between the antler-bare trees and read the true lay of the land, the rise and fall of it, to review contours and landforms visible only in this brief season of abeyance between snowmelt and leaf-sprout.

This is also the season of rediscovery—of the busted snow shovel, the flattened chicken feed bags, the leaves you never raked last fall (now pressed against the earth like baked potato skin), the mouse you took from the trap and flung into the yard that night last January when it was twenty below. When I lost a brand-new steel shoe off my snowplow while clearing this winter's first big blizzard, I knew my only chance of recovering it lay in this narrow window of time, and indeed last week I retraced my route on foot until I found the part on the freshly bared ground, the price tag still in place. I felt like I had won thirty-four dollars in the lottery.

Soon the revivifying sun will turn loose summer. The green things will rise up and take over. While passing through Appleton I spotted a cluster of pale purple flowers in a yard. It was as visually surprising as if someone had scattered the ground with pastel candies. The blooms looked so colorfully *alive,* but still—perhaps with an eye toward the last grainy slush crystals over there along the back of the garage—they stayed tight to the ground, not willing to stick their necks out *too* far.

FACTS AND FANTICIES

There used to be, on the east side of Highway 27 somewhere north of Holcombe and south of Ladysmith, a building that may have been an old gas station or may have been just an old house, but was eye-catching in that it displayed a large yellow sign with spray-painted letters declaring FACTS AND FANCIES on one side and FACTS AND FANTICIES on the other.

I may not have the spelling exactly right, but then neither did they.

I thought of this mystery business during a recent trip north on 27. It was a day of sun and melt, a false spring that we nonetheless take at its word, happily allowing ourselves to be fooled, so hungry for warmth are we. "Is it spring, Daddy?" asked my younger child, and I said, "No, but act like it is." Just south of the Holcombe Flowage I spotted a flotilla of shrink-wrapped pontoon boats beached behind a chain-link fence, as sure a sign as any that the season of open water was still a ways off.

Warmth aside, I think I can say without giving offense that things in that part of the state look pretty rawbone on days like this. Bright sun bouncing off the residual white crust illuminates the countryside filter-free between the naked trees, revealing abandoned shacks, sagging siding, a stash of cracked rubber tires, old pickup trucks parked forlornly by the ditch with FOR SALE signs propped on the dash, and once, in a ravine, some unidentified flywheeled contraption, all cast iron and rivets, abandoned in another age, the price of scrap never quite overcoming its difficult location and mass. It was in this reflective mood that I kept an eye out for FACTS AND FANCIES/FANTICIES, but unless I missed it, the building seems to have been burned or bulldozed.

Back in the day, I never had the guts to stop in and find out exactly what was available. I can certainly understand why someone might sell "FANCIES," which covers pretty much everything from jewelry to lace. As for "FANTICIES," well, whether we're talking politics or second shift at the Bunny Ranch, the market has always been bullish.

What really has me flummoxed is the "FACTS." Which facts? Whose facts? And what about that stretch of highway made the erstwhile proprietor think folks might be running low on verifiable information? You'll note the sign didn't say *trivia*. These people were dealing in *FACTS*. Solid stuff, like the specific gravity of mercury, or the composition of chert rock, or the height of the Cornell stacker.

But I blew my chances and will never know. Instead, as I drove along I settled for my own imaginary scene, in which a lonely traveler pulls into the lot, looks at the sign, and walks inside. "Can I help you?" says a burly man behind the counter. "Yes," says the customer, "one fact, and one fantasy, please." At which point the burly man barks out, "Lima is the capital of Peru!," produces a feather duster, and gives the customer a hearty spank.

I could be wrong. But the idea of it kept me giggling all the way to Highway 8.

ISLAND LIFE

I had just settled in at the Red Cup Coffee House when the electricity failed. It was an overcast morning and summer traffic to Washington Island was on the wane, so the room was populated largely by regulars. After a brief pause in the chatter, there came a chuckle of recognition, as if the power failure was but another familiar friend stepping through the door. Then everyone resumed talking in the dark.

I like to think of Washington Island as the dot completing the inverted exclamation point of the Door County peninsula. As I rode the ferry across Death's Door, I was reminded (as I also am when I visit places like Bayfield, or Green Bay, or Superior, or Manitowoc, or Algoma) how easy it is for those of us raised in the landlocked cows-and-corn portions of Wisconsin to forget about the maritime fringes of the state. I always feel as if I'm sneaking a visit to the East Coast on the cheap, except out there you can't get a cheese curd with your seagull.

The denizens of Washington Island have graciously hosted my family several times off and on over the years in order that I might sing some songs or yap about my books. One winter we holed up on the island for the better part of a month while I hacked away at the opening chapters of a book about love and old pickup trucks—often while sitting in a corner of the Red Cup Coffee House. Our last visit was five years ago, so it was delightful to step inside the shop this past week and feel as if I had stepped out only the previous afternoon. Owners Mike and Ann were still in place behind the counter, assisted by their daughter, Tate. Over the years Mike has become known for what might be described as a "forthright" customer service model, and it was reassuring to find that he still seemed a tad grumpy, which I took as a testament to the consistency of his character. For the first time in thirteen years, Mike and Ann will close up shop over the winter. They'll reopen come spring, but I expect a few desperate decaffeinated locals will be found frozen to the coffee shop windows before the thaw.

I was facing a writing deadline, so I set up at a table along the wall. While the laptop woke itself I was pleased to note I recognized a few familiar faces among the post-summer crew convened at an adjacent table. As when I last visited, they were discussing the state of the world. It was unanimously agreed that there was room for improvement, and several suggestions were made to that end. Action, on the other hand, was tabled in favor of a refill and further review.

Memory has a way of fooling us, so I was grateful to take a first pull on my coffee and find it every bit as good as I remembered. My standards in most things run about ankle high, but over time and travel I have morphed into a closet coffee snob. The stuff at the Red Cup rates my highest category: So good, that first sip makes me wanna flop over and shake my leg like a belly-scratched dog.

I had been writing for half an hour when the lights went out. The power returned briefly at one point, then everything went dark again. By now it felt nice that way and I had plenty of battery, so I kept writing. I heard one of the regulars say, "Well, as soon as the power goes off the valve shuts, so you don't have to worry about that," but all other conversation addressed everything but the lack of juice. Island life breeds a certain level of acceptance, and it was lovely—even under deadline—to absorb a bit of that by osmosis.

When the power sparked on the second time, it stayed on. The lights came up just as one of the locals stepped through the door. She was rewarded with a hearty round of applause, after which could be heard the sound of the coffee grinder and more conversation.

CREEPING CODGERISM

SELFIE STICK

We have lately observed the proliferation of that simplest of twenty-first-century tools known as the "selfie stick," which holds your cellphone at a distance, thus allowing you to shoot self-portraits as your social media stream deems and demands. While I have dismissively referred to the selfie stick as emblematic of the society of self-indulgent self-regard (says the guy who has written four books about himself), last week I changed my stance.

The motivation for both my dislike and my change of heart has to do with chronology, particularly my own. Having recently crossed the half-century line, I am well into that stage of life that can only be classified as creeping codgerism, in which all the follies of the world are framed in my figurative porch window—whereas my own follies are too close to be clearly seen now that my eyes won't focus on anything more proximal than my fully extended arms.

As the term implies, creeping codgerism transpires over minuscule increments. You don't just roll out of bed one day fully dyspeptic and out of touch. (In fact, your days of "rolling" out of bed are numbered, if this morning's joint-popping groan-fest was any indication; envision a wincing stick insect disentangling itself from a flannel cocoon and shuffling off puffy-eyed to the bathroom.) No, there are little moments: Your daughter returns from a field trip to Chicago brimming with stories and knowledge, and you are pleased for her but confused when she insists on referring to the tallest building in the Windy City as the "Willis

Tower," when you know for a fact it is the Sears. Or, while on your way to the bathroom you hear the man on TV say, "Would you like thicker, more luscious hair?" and your inner voice replies by reflex, *Well, sure,* but by the time you find the bathroom mirror you realize there are other issues and your inner voice has lost all conviction. Or, along comes something like a selfie stick, and you realize: The earth is shifting beneath my feet, and I don't care to dance.

And this is where you have to put in some extra effort, lest creeping codgerism—which has its own grumpy charm and furthermore excuses you from caring about things like the Top Forty and whether bell bottoms are in or out—becomes ingrown decrepitude. And so it was that last week, after receiving a text message while running errands only to discover that I had left the car without any reading glasses (verified after three rounds of the "pat-your-pockets, pat-your-head" confirmation dance) and then struggling to extend my arm far enough so that I might decipher the content of the message, that I realized: What I need is a selfie stick! Not to take my own dang picture, but to place my phone at readable distance.

As you might expect, I have contacted the leading selfie stick manufacturers proposing a new marketing plan incorporating my insights and targeting the codger demographic. Soon the money will be rolling in. I will use the cash to buy a selfie stick and take pictures of my brand-new thicker, more luscious hair.

IMPERFECT

Lately I have been considering life's imperfections. These ruminations generally commence in the morning, which is to say, the moment I face the mirror.

Things are falling apart apace. The ol' jawline isn't what it once was, the lines bracketing my chin look ever more like those of a human nutcracker or ventriloquist's mannequin, and you could plant pine seedlings in the twin furrows cleaving what should be my two eyebrows. (Only once have I had two eyebrows, and that was after a woman in a French hair salon on New York City's Upper East Side attacked me with a tweezers in a manner possibly violating the Geneva Convention. I was conducting what some in the trade call "participatory journalism" at the time, although when I tried to explain that down to the fire hall, no one would listen.)

There are upshots to my physical decline, chief among them my retirement plan, which is based on investing the money I'm saving on hair care products, as my annual needs are easily satisfied—and even exceeded—by harvesting motel mini-shampoos during book tour. I generate additional dividends by serving as my own barber. At this point it is less like giving myself a haircut and more like mowing the weeds on a vacant lot. Occasionally this plan leads to my emerging in public with an accidental strip of occipital fuzz, but I can't see it, so it doesn't really bother me, and besides, most people are so distracted by my single eyebrow they never really notice the back of my head.

Sadly, whatever time I have saved by the recession of the hair adorning my dome is being more than consumed by all the trimming and pruning required to keep at bay hair that is paradoxically thriving, specifically that sprouting from my nose, ears, and eyebrows. There is some sort of inversely proportional thing happening here, and I could do three paragraphs on the phenomenon, but some of you may be trying to eat breakfast.

Finally, it takes longer to shave these days. Oh, I still lather up and scrape my face in the same amount of time as ever—but that's only the *first* shave. Because at my age, after the *first* shave, you have to put on your reading glasses and—quickly, before they fog up—check out all the spots you missed because you can no longer actually see individual whiskers. It's that *second* shave that fools the world into thinking you're doing fine with "activities of daily living" and keeps your family from sitting you down for "the talk."

Later today, I'm giving myself another selfie haircut, because I have to go speak in public and it's been a couple of weeks since the last trim. My scalp has taken on the appearance of a late-stage anemic dandelion. My hair is neither long nor short, creating a look that floats somewhere between uncommitted nutty professor and dissolute drill sergeant. I'll lose a little time with the clippers, as well as the requisite ear, nose, and eyebrow hedge trimming, but I'm going to make it up with a swift mini-shampoo and by skipping the two-stage shave completely. I usually do, this time of year. I can grow a decent—if not voluminous—beard, and whatever it may or may not do for my looks, it does guard the cheeks and chin against the cutting winds of cold to come. Also, with each passing year it resembles more and more the snow, a useful form of camouflage should it come to that. And while we're on the topic of camouflage, the beard eases those morning mirror sessions by obscuring any unhappy jawline developments or exacerbated nutcracker-face.

Of course this leaves the twin furrows. Perhaps if they become overly worrisome I can let the eyebrows go and perform some sort of unibrow comb-over.

Then, next time I'm on the Upper East Side, I'll go scare the tweezer lady.

COLD CHARACTER

I hesitate to be judgmental, so: *one-thousand-one, one-thousand-two, one-thousand-three.* There. Now let's talk about people who bail out on winter.

I have long harbored an abiding distrust of Midwesterners who lack the moral fiber to stand their ground in the face of blizzards and black ice. Those noodle-spined surrender-bathers who trade snow and subzero for sun and sand, leaving the rest of us stuck here like some kid who licked the monkey bars in January. I am aware that a flagpole would be more culturally iconic, but I have never licked a flagpole. Whereas the monkey bars—well, I didn't *lick* them, but I did lick my upper lip before leaning in to see how close I could get without making contact (Estimated Distance minus One Millimeter, as it turned out), and I can tell you that a detached patch of frozen lip epidermis flutters in the frigid wind like parchment paper in a drafty deep freeze. Also, you will want to avoid salt-and-vinegar potato chips for a solid forty-eight hours.

I will judge, but I won't forbid. If you want to trade your snowshoes for sandals, well, go for it. You do what you think you *need* to do, I say, in a tone of voice I learned from my mother right before I bought my first—and last—Speedo. Go on and frolic in the surf while leaving the rest of us stuck hip deep in a snowbank—if that's what you think you *need* to do. As for me, I operate (as best one can while stuck hip deep in a snowbank) within a sterner code. I shudder to think of the state of my body and soul if I could simply open the door and stroll outside all barefooted willy-nilly without first spending a good twenty minutes performing the mental and physical calisthenics necessary to clothe myself in a series of overlapping and mismatched layers, including a pair of abrasive wool long johns that haven't fit right for at least fifteen pounds now. How slight of character would I be if my plow truck was a tropical jet ski that started on the first try and I didn't have to genuflect before the frosted battery charger, or prostrate myself in shivering humility beneath the crankcase while trying to attach the pan heater as my butt cheeks chilled to lard through six layers of thermal futility.

In short, cold builds character. The sort of character that yields a guy like me. A man driven by a deep sense of duty. A man who, when his mother-in-law asks if he can house-sit, puts aside all other commitments and puts himself in service. Of course I had to rearrange my work schedule and there were certain logistical inconveniences, but this is the kind of thing a duty-driven son-in-law does without complaint.

I am there now. On duty. The house in question is nothing fancy. A modest single-story stucco, with a simple porch. It is built into a low foothill and is approachable only by a potholed gravel road.

Also, it overlooks the Caribbean.

I am disoriented by the scent of sunscreen in January. The distant water is travel-brochure blue and accessible with flipflops, rather than a motorized ice auger. I breathe deeply the breeze, and my nostrils don't freeze shut. Over on the far side of the pool (such *sloth!*), an iguana drops from the hedge and commences a slow circuit of the deck. He is the size of a squirrel with a foot-long tail and skin the color of neon avocado flesh. Parking himself in the sun, he scratches his head with one claw, then stares at me, sitting there typing in my non-Speedo.

"Working!" I say. *"Duty!"* I add, perhaps a tad frantically.

The iguana is impassive. We have a staring contest. I hang in there, but lose when I have to blink away the tears arising when

I realize how much snow I'm gonna have to shovel to atone for my desertion and sunshiny backsliding.

The iguana climbs the knee wall. Just before he disappears into the tamarind trees, he pauses to look back over his shoulder, and—perhaps it was the sunstroke, but I swear—speaks.

"You do what you think you *need* to do."

YOGA BRANDING

Recently a real live yogi asked my wife and me for help renaming his yoga studio. Asking a guy like me to rename your yoga studio is the rough equivalent of asking a room full of teenaged boys to come up with an advertising slogan for baked beans, but I agreed to do the best I could, which is to say we lowered the bar immediately.

This all came about in the first place because my wife is a longtime student of the yogic arts. I don't know if they give out yogi belts like they do karate belts, but if they did I guess my wife would be somewhere at the higher end, say a third-degree rainbow belt or a first degree tie-dye. She was studying before I met her (as a matter of fact, in the department of "Hey! Who's Creepy?," she was doing yoga in the first photo I ever Googled of her) and sustains a dedicated practice to this day. Over the past several years she has been studying with the yogi in question, and he's become a family friend. In fact, we've had him over for pancakes. Gluten-free quinoa pancakes sprinkled with essence of dandelion, or something along those righteous nutritional lines, but nonetheless I think you should know that even yogis like pancakes.

I have all the flexibility of a narrow-minded scarecrow, so both my wife and the yogi have tried to get me to try a few poses over the years, but it hasn't gone well. For one thing, I comport myself upon the mat with all the grace of a concussed cow. For another, yoga requires patience, dedication, and follow-through, and I just don't think that's fair.

Nonetheless, my wife hangs in there. One thing I admire about her as a yoga instructor is her dedication to sharing the benefits of yoga with groups of people not normally considered yoga-friendly. For instance, a year or two ago she asked me to help her write some promotional materials designed to lure farmers into attending yoga classes. I was pretty skeptical at first, until I started paging through one of my wife's textbooks and discovered many of the poses were directly applicable. For instance, you've got your plow pose, otherwise known as halasana. You've got your wheel pose, which looks to me like it'd be a good choice if you were trying to locate a grease zerk on the underside of the hay baler. You've got your Seated Wide Legged Straddle, otherwise known as upavistha konasana, which would come in handy when dismounting from the tractor or avoiding a charging pig. Then there's Awkward Chair Pose, which I would call the Uff-Da, and half-moon pose, which I renamed Farmer Dropped His Pliers. (Some might call it The Plumber.)

I wrote these suggestions up and shared them with my wife, because we are in this together, whether she likes it or not. After reading them, she looked at me in a manner betraying the fact that she has a *looong* way to go on this whole inner peace thing. Nonetheless, when the yogi called for help renaming his studio, she asked if I had any ideas. After a period of reflection coming in at just under three minutes, I compiled the following list: Languid Yoga. Grunty Yoga. Slippery Yoga. Do We Hafta Yoga. Something Popped Yoga. Oops Yoga. OK Yoga. Holy Yogi Yoga. Nice Tights Yoga. The Yoga Barn. Old Country Yoga Buffet. Posing 4 Posers. Dude-i-o with a Studio. And finally: Rock Hard in Your Leotard.

I submitted the list for review, but didn't hear back. When I inquired, my wife said she hadn't found time to respond because she's been busy developing a new yoga pose especially for me. She says she hasn't decided what to call it yet. She's leaning toward Sound of One Hamstring Snapping, but for the sake of brevity may go with The Trussed Turkey.

ORTHODONTIST

You will know if you have seen me smile that I have never lingered long in the company of orthodontists. Over time my teeth have proven to be serviceable and strong, but cosmetically speaking, they are a motley assemblage. Right up front and off-center, one incisor is askew and getting askewer, the misalignment highlighted by a corner knocked loose in grade school when the local banker's daughter eliminated me from a game of dodgeball with an overhand howitzer shot that I'm certain bumped her up three spots in the NFL draft. I tasted smoke, spit chips, and felt a nascent shift in my heretofore naïve certitudes with respect to established gender roles in a patriarchal society.

The most prominent feature of my dentition is a front-and-center gap that will allow the passage of one thin dime, or a nickel in hard times. The official name for the space is *diastema,* and when I was young my parents asked if I wanted to get it fixed, but by then I had honed an ability to spit water through the diastema to a remarkable distance and with enough force to knock a cabbage moth from the air. This was the childhood equivalent of a superpower, and I wasn't about to give it up. It got to where I could spritz my brother in the back of the head from fifteen paces. I don't do that anymore, as he is all grown up and a logger. His diastema is even larger than mine—as a matter of fact all three of we brothers sport one. Once I ordered T-shirts for each of us that said, "I'M GAP-TOOTHED, AND I VOTE!" On a possibly related note, all three of we fellows were into our thirties before we found wives.

I am married now, with two daughters, the elder of whom has long been afflicted with a wayward bicuspid and moderate jaw alignment issues, and so when she hit her teen years we joined the orthodontia brigade. My wife and daughter interviewed several orthodontists, finally selecting one with good references and a flexible payment plan. My only reservation lay in the fact that when I met him he appeared to be twelve years old. I run into this a lot now that I'm of a certain age, and my daughter informs me he is actually married and has two daughters of his own, but it is all I can do to keep myself from telling him not to spend all our money on skateboards and bubble gum.

And he does have our money. Until I go to my grave, every time I see my daughter smile I will recall the instant when I wrote that breathtaking check. It was, in the most etymologic sense, your classic bracing moment. I submit this without complaint, as we are nearing the final visit and the results have been nothing short of remarkable. I do not begrudge the orthodontist his fee. That said, the first time I visited his clinic, I noted he shares an office suite with a financial adviser. In light of the one direction money flows between us I don't know if this is kismet for him or irony for me.

At her next appointment, my daughter will have her braces removed. As much as she has enjoyed sporting a mouthful of multicolored rubber bands, she tells me she is eager to be free of the wires. It will be lovely to see her fresh smile, the rogue tooth brought into line, the malocclusions resolved. And if she smiles beside me, her teeth will look even more perfect by comparison. I could join her, I suppose. More and more adults are mingling with the teenagers in the waiting rooms these days. But no—I shall maintain my gap. Not ready to write that check, for starters. But also not willing to surrender my superpower. A full-grown man shouldn't be doing things like knocking horseflies off a rock using nothing but a swig of water and a diastema, but when I do, my girls giggle and grin and that's all the perfect smile I need.

DISHWASHER

Sometimes a guy has to step forward and take the lead on the important issues of the day, and so I finally called a family meeting the other night for the purposes of discussing new dishwasher distribution directives. Some say I just stood there in my ugly pilled slippers and grumbled to myself while holding a dirty fork.

As luxuries go, I rank automatic dishwashers right up there. In part this is due to a life lived largely without the appliance. For a brief time during my childhood my mother had one, a big boxy model on wheels with a hose that hooked to the kitchen faucet. When it broke, Mom replaced it with us. This wasn't so bad, because we had a large family, so there were a lot of off days in the rotation.

For a single year after college I rented an apartment with an automatic dishwasher and reveled in the simplicity of putting dishes in dirty and taking them out clean. During this time I developed the preliminary elements of my "pre-rinse versus post-rinse" principles, about which more later. I also learned what happens when you put ordinary dishwashing liquid into an automatic dishwasher. As I shoveled suds into the sink with a cake pan, I swore I'd never make that mistake again.

There followed a fifteen-year stretch of dishwasherless bachelorhood, during which time I maintained a rigorous regimen of doing the dishes every time I found myself eating oatmeal from the gravy boat.

Finally I married, and we moved to a house with a dishwasher.

This has allowed me to update and refine my dishwasher-loading techniques. I have developed a few time-saving tricks, including the one where I load the silverware basket by shooting the utensils in handle-first. It's like playing vertical darts, or flatware mumblety-peg, and the upside is, rather than bending over to place every piece of silverware, you only have to bend over to pick up the ones that miss. Economy of time and motion, pal, that's the secret to good living.

I also save a lot of time by refusing to pre-rinse. *Oh, you must pre-rinse,* everyone says. Really? I chuckle. How perfectly backward. My studies show that over 90 percent of all dishes will clean up just fine without rinsing. That's a lot of superfluous rinsing. *Wash* first, then you'll *know* which plates needed rinsing. Yes, I hear you saying, but have you ever tried scraping egg yolk off after it's been baked on in the dishwasher? To which I reply, have you ever tried *rinsing* egg yolk off a plate? You'll end up handwashing it anyway.

In our present situation, all four members of our family share in the loading and unloading duties, which is to say it is impossible for me to ignore the shortcomings of the others. First of all, I observe frequent violations of the Dish Density Factor, in which dishes of different sizes are racked in willy-nilly proximity, resulting in gaps and poor space management. Rigorous attention to uniform nesting (ordered by ascending diameter and convexity) calms my nerves and soothes my nascent OCD, although the woman who steps over my dirty socks every morning finds my concern curious. Aesthetics aside, Dish Density also enables speed-unloading, in which I grab up to eight plates at once and hardly ever drop any. If you still aren't convinced, the Dish Density Factor can be defended strictly in terms of conservation. When there is more unoccupied space, the ratio of water used to dishes washed gets all out of whack and somewhere a penguin dies.

I gave a speech about this during that impromptu family

meeting the other night. After which I inadvertently filled the detergent dispenser with regular dish soap and discovered it is difficult to maintain a position of authority while shoveling four cubic feet of suds into the sink with a cake pan.

DOORMAN

The parking lot was unusually crowded and we noticed lot of Minnesota plates when I delivered the eight-year-old to her swimming lesson in the middle school natatorium last weekend. (I had to memorize *natatorium* for a spelling bee once, so I want to get some mileage out of it.) As it turned out all the congestion was due to a basketball tournament in progress.

After the youngster was in the pool, I searched for a flat surface where I might spread out paperwork and a laptop to get some work done, and found the perfect spot at an empty countertop directly facing the school entryway. I arranged my materials and had just begun to review a document when a young basketball player approached and asked where the restrooms were. I pointed down the hallway and got back to work, only to be interrupted by someone asking me a question about the tournament schedule. I explained that I wasn't actually affiliated with the tournament and pointed hopefully down another hallway where I'd heard basketball noises (this is not my daughter's school, and I am unfamiliar with the layout). The next person who walked up to the counter pulled out his wallet and said, "How much?"

I explained that I wasn't selling tickets. Right about then another couple walked through the doors and, before veering off toward the basketball sounds, raised and rotated their arms so I could see that their hands had been stamped.

I just gave them the nod.

It's not that I looked official. I was wearing an old camo cap and a Packers hoodie. My power was completely location-based. That counter between me and the door was the furniture equivalent of a pen and clipboard, which even in this digital age can gain you access to pretty much any place short of the nuclear launch room.

It was a heady moment. I was tempted to use my power for my own entertainment. What fun it would be, rather than giving directions to the B-Bracket, to play dumb and provide alternatives:

"Don't know, but the carp-shooting clinic commences at the deep end of the pool in five minutes."

"Got me, but I highly recommend the first aid and taxidermy workshop—five bucks, and that includes platelets and a complimentary live badger."

"Sorry, you're at the wrong school. What we got going here today is full-contact knitting. The needles you can rent, but the steel wool you gotta pay for."

"Tournament's canceled. May I recommend my pal Goober's 401(k) investment seminar? Starts in twenty minutes at the far end of the high dive, right after they drain the pool."

Wimpy me, my imagination exceeds my courage. For the remainder of the hour I pecked away at my work, nodding in approval at the hand-stamp flashers, pointing out the restrooms, politely refusing cash, and when all else failed, outright admitting that I was nothing more than a dad with no authority.

From now on I'm bringing a cash box, a stamp kit, and a roll of tickets. By the time that eight-year-old masters the butterfly, we'll have the college fund all set.

PEAK WALTER MITTY

July is drawing to a close, and I have hit peak Walter Mitty.

Those of you familiar with the overdreaming, underachieving Thurber character would have recognized him in me during the months of April and May as I strode about the property pointing out this project and that project, and listing my plans to execute same: In yonder pole barn I shall rearrange the lumber in order to clear space for the clubhouse I will build for the children right after I get the ol' International pickup truck running again so that I can use it to haul all the firewood I will split after repairing the chainsaw in order to trim the limb that is rubbing on the shingles over on the side of the house where I intend to replace the storm window that threatens to fall from the frame of its own accord and land atop the gutters I will clean first thing tomorrow morning unless I decide to finally hang the laying boxes I got off FreeCycle five years ago, although before I do that I shall fix the iffy latch on the coop door, although this reminds me I have yet to build that chicken tractor I dreamed up, the one that will be the envy of the poultry world and will incorporate the running gear with the flat tire that needs to be pulled and patched before I can rearrange things in order to get at the pile of salvaged wooden doors that need to be shifted so I can reach and remove the folded stack of silage plastic covering the vintage hovercraft in order to finally shoot the photos I need to post it for sale on Craigslist, and well, whoops, looky here, July is a spent squib, August is in sight, and still the list exists.

The thing is, in my Mitty mind, I *have* rearranged the lumber. I *have* fixed that window. I *have* sold that hovercraft. *Visualize* success, the motivational experts say, and boy, do I ever. And yet that window still hangs crazily askew, no one has bid on the hovercraft because I still haven't posted it, and as of last week I note there are maple seedlings sprouting from the gutters.

Oh, there have been some partial victories: The woodshed is a shade over half full, and there is enough seasoned wood on hand elsewhere to finish the job and get us through winter. The maple trees are trimmed, although honesty compels me to admit I had a little bit of help there from a crew of fellows who showed up with their own chainsaws, a truck with a boom and bucket, a howling wood chipper, and a bill, which they left me when they finished.

I did hang those laying boxes.

And although I haven't got beyond *visualizing* the clubhouse, I did take my daughters fishing. Just once, but it was a good day. Sunny, warm, breezy, and bug-free. We only caught a couple, and they were real small, but the smiles were real big. Sometimes it feels good to do something that wasn't on the list.

So here comes August, and I can't stop it. I haven't given up—there are now photos of a vintage hovercraft on my phone—but I have begun to relax my standards. I recognize the pattern. I've lived it before. It's that stage when the peak Walter Mitty version of me looks around, does the math, shrugs his shoulders, and adjusts his priorities precipitously downward. The stage, in other words, when Walter Mitty becomes Walter *Mitigate*.

But go ahead and put that hovercraft on your watch list. It'll show up eventually. In my mind, it's posted already.

FOUND IT

For over forty years, my father shepherded a flock of sheep. After he sold the last of them, he cleaned out his vet cupboard and handed me his hoof trimmers. I flipped the leather loop free and the handles sprang open. I worked them a time or two. The blades were still surgically sharp and met with airtight precision. I hadn't wielded the tool for twenty years, but the drop-forged steel sat in my palm with a familiar heft and set loose a rush of recollection.

We trimmed the sheep's hooves once in the warmer months when we wormed them, and once before lambing season when we sheared them. Dad turned this task over to me early, and it was one of those quiet rite of passage deals that square a boy's shoulders. Wrassling the sheep around til it was sitting on its hind end propped between my knees, I raised the hooves one by one, inspecting each claw (as indeed the cleft sections are called) for those areas where the hoof wall had overgrown and curled under like a bad Frito. Then I'd fish the trimmers out of my back pants pocket, flip the riveted leather retaining loop loose so the handles could spring open, carefully cut away the excess horn to properly expose the sole, and finish off by pruning the toe tip so once again the sheep was walking square with the earth. To watch a freshly pedicured ewe bolt freely back to pasture made a young boy feel he'd done something useful. I secured the trimmers in the closed position, thanked Dad, took them home, and hung them on a hook down in the pole barn.

Some time later I was struggling to trim the wing feathers of a wayward chicken. I was using a cheap pair of scissors and it was slow going. On a whim I decided to try the hoof trimmers. *Snick-snick,* and the job was done, neat as you please. The next time I saw Dad, it was fun to tell him the old nippers were back in business.

This past spring varmint-related circumstances required me to barber the feathers of sixty-two chickens. Thanks to those hoof trimmers the first sixty-one were done in a trice. (Well, not a trice. You don't trim the wings of sixty-one chickens in a trice, even with top-grade shears. There was dander and cackling and the chickens got worked up too.) But Chicken Number 62 escaped. *No problem,* I thought, *it'll come home to roost and I'll catch it in the morning.*

Trouble was, come sunup and I had Chicken Number 62 in hand, I couldn't find the hoof trimmers. They weren't on the hook where they belonged, or in the granary where the cheap scissors hung, or on the workbench, or visible anywhere in the coop. I racked my brain trying to remember where I might have left them. Finally I figured I must have set them on the windowsill of the coop and they got knocked off into what polite people call "chicken litter." There followed a difficult half an hour in which I sifted through several wheelbarrowsful of "litter." Nothing. I finally gave up and trimmed the chicken with the bad scissors.

Summer passed. Leaves dropped, snow fell, deer hunting season came and went, and it was time to make venison sausage. In search of some extra pails for trimmings, I went down to the pole barn and pulled a green bucket from a shelf. Something clunked within. I looked, and there were the hoof trimmers.

For the life of me I couldn't recall what sort of absentminded meandering might have led me to drop the trimmers in a bucket and then completely forget I'd done so. These are the moments where a guy wonders if he should be trusted with keeping track of his own socks, let alone children or a bank account. *But aha,* I thought. *I know a memory trick!* Balancing the trimmers on my palm, I closed my eyes, vibed on the heft, and waited for the sweet rush of recollection. Nothing. Then I tried it while clutching the bucket. Again, nothing, although I did work up a cramp between my eyebrows right where the furrows converge.

It strikes me lately that perhaps the chickens are involved. They have motive. In the meantime, I hung the hoof trimmers on the hook, right where I can find them.

At least I think I did.

Did I ever tell you my dad had sheep?

FIXING THE TUBELESS TIRE

Last week I was brush-hogging the burdock and wild cucumber that are lately threatening to overtake our farm. They have become the kudzu of the north, and I look forward to the day when automobiles are powered by burdock and wild cucumber juice because the money will roll in at such a rate I'll be laughing at all of you while reclining in my own personal private Lambeau Field skybox as stout Midwestern maidens dressed in blaze orange teddies hand-feed me deep-fried cheese curds and run their fingers through my gorgeous new hair.

I have my dreams, you have yours.

When I climbed aboard the tractor I noticed the left front tire was low. A responsible operator would have ceased operations immediately and pumped up the tire, but I had no time for maintenance or common sense. Shortly thereafter I hit a bump and heard a sound evocative of an elephant squatting on a dodgeball. When I looked down, the low tire was now flat and all mashed over to one side.

There followed a moment of reflection and introspection, during which I gave close consideration to the temper of my intellect, the state of my spirit, and my predilection for terminal dunderheadedness. Scores were low in every category but the last.

When you knock a tubeless tractor tire off the bead, you can't simply reinflate the inner tube as you might on your bike. You have to reestablish the seal between the tire and the rim—and it isn't easy. Plus, do it wrong, and you'll put a tire tool through your cranium. There are tricks to doing it right. Tricks your average reflective essayist does not possess—even if he *is* wearing boots and a camo cap. Plus I'm not good with tools. I'm the kind of guy who takes an emotional victory lap after successfully changing out the cartridge in my laser printer.

I called my brothers Jed and John. They own big tractors and log forwarders and dump trucks, all fitted with gigantic tubeless tires. My brothers are used to these kinds of calls. They smile indulgently as they explain yet again how to hook up the battery charger, or sharpen the chainsaw chain, or why maybe I shouldn't try to change my own oil. You can hear in their voices that they think it's fortunate and cute that I learned how to type.

We wound up playing phone tag, but eventually both Jed and John left me a voice mail with tubeless tire–mounting tips. John's message was the most comprehensive. I shan't go into all the specifics, but I can tell you that in the course of a sixty-second recording he made reference to a can of ether, a handful of black powder, the scent of burning rubber, a logging chain, a propane tank, and right at the end there, a tomato cannon. I think he meant potato cannon, but why quibble. Just before he hung up, he said, "Leave your head on."

My brother Jed's message was much shorter. He said I'd probably have to take the tire to town to get it fixed. Or, as he put it, "It's called shut up and shell out." Which is pretty much what I figured.

One of the essential subelements of terminal dunderheadedness is unrehabilitative stubbornness. Against all odds and sense, I pulled the tire, joggled and wrassled it around to get it seated as best I could (a process similar to massaging a mortified alligator), and hit it with a blast of air. For the first little bit nothing happened. I joggled the tire some more and tried again. And just when I was ready to "shut up and shell out," I heard the sweetest echoey *ping* as the bead seated against the rim. This was followed by more pings and stretchy rubbery sounds as the tire refilled and resumed its usable form.

I am not a dancing man, but if I coulda, I woulda. Do you understand the status I am now accorded? Me walking down the street and women and children and men alike, turning to whisper, "That man right there, he can mount a tubeless tractor tire."

I'll be seeing my brothers at Sunday dinner one of these days. I'm gonna puff up my chest and tell 'em I got that tire back on all by myself.

And they'll look at me, sitting there all proud as a kindergartner who drew a lopsided turkey by tracing his soft little hand, and they'll know I'll never be able to do it again in a million years, and they'll say, "What a nice story. You oughta type that right up."

TAPE MEASURE STORY

At last count, I owned seven tape measures. As with reading glasses, you can never find one when you need one, so I buy them in bulk and scatter them everywhere.

In order to stretch my tape measure budget, I draw a fine line between quality and economy. Once while shopping for materials to build a modest hunting shack I found myself in a well-known home improvement chain store staring at a hot pink tape measure. I liked the idea of the pink tape measure not because pink's my thing but because I figured it would be easy to find if I ever I misplaced it, which usually happens about five minutes into the project. I waffled a bit, because the tape measure cost $1.95, and if you buy a twenty-five-foot tape measure for under two bucks you are buying junk and you know it, but then I thought, *Well, what the heck because it's not like I need something top of the line and as a matter of fact with my limited carpenter skills a high-end tape measure seems an overoptimistic investment.* And so I bought the thing.

The very first time I tried to use it, while measuring corner to corner to make sure the wall I was building was square (it wasn't), the tape was extended about eight feet when the tab slipped off the board and the blade retracted, *z-whup!* It whipped around some at the end there, and because the blade was made of an unidentified metal one notch below tinfoil, the force of the retraction put a kink in it, the upshot being that the end of the blade curved up and every time I hooked it over a board and tried to take a measurement, the end sprung loose and *z-whup!* rolled itself up. The third time this happened, I rose up to my tiptoes and hurled the thing straight down with all the fury I could muster.

When it hit the floorboards, the tape measure exploded like a cheap . . . tape measure. The hot pink shell split in two halves. One half flew out into an adjacent overgrown pasture. The other half bounded nearly straight up and landed on the roof of my father's woodshed. The tape, released from the confines of the case, uncoiled with explosive force, flinging itself every which way. I cannot lie, it was a most satisfying result. There are more acceptable ways to handle blind rage, but show me one that pays off with the same level of instant gratification.

That's what you get for buying a $1.95 tape measure, I thought, and immediately felt the rage returning. Sure, my fault, but they knew that tape measure was a piece of junk when they put it on the shelf. It was fraudulent at any price. I couldn't find the one half that had bounced into the cow yard, but I got the other off the roof, wrapped the blade around it in a big wad, taped the whole works together into a shattered, twisted bundle, and headed back to the store. When I got there I went to the customer service counter and using my best *I'm about to climb a tall tower with a big gun* gaze, looked the nice young lady square in the eyes, held out the clustered remnants, and said two words.

"This broke."

She looked at the wad of wreckage. Then she looked back at me.

Then she dug $1.95 out of the till.

I used the money to buy nails I couldn't hit.

FREELANCE SNIFFER

In August of 2006, the *New York Times* announced the appointment of fragrance expert Chandler Burr as its first-ever perfume critic, and I am still jealous. I really wanted that gig.

Let me be clear: Mr. Burr was the right man for the job. I shall never forget his characterization of Sel de Vétiver as "unearthly as a god born in the cold." That's not the kind of phrase you hear every day, at least not down to the feed mill or fire hall, where the similes—while vivid and equally cherished—tend to run a tad closer to the ground.

If the *Times* had chosen me, my first order of business would have been to expand the job description beyond twee distillations the rest of us can't afford until Wal-Mart does the knockoff. (In fairness to Chandler Burr, let it be known he once gave high marks to a bottle of Coppertone suntan lotion and parsed the fragrance of New York City asphalt.) The world is full of aromas not contained in sculpted decanters that nonetheless cry out for review. As such, I wish to offer my services—to the *New York Times,* sure, but also to humankind—as a second-tier olfactory journalist. A guy willing to go beyond Chanel No. 5 and deconstruct scents for those of us who tend to favor fragrances along the lines of smelt, fresh axle grease, and damp fire hose.

I offer as my qualifications a wide range of scent-based experience, including but not limited to a firsthand familiarity with the smell of fear, whiffs of desperation, secondhand pepper spray, and the redolence of overserved frat boys. While my early train-ing (completed within a six-square-mile patch of northern Chip-pewa County, Wisconsin) focused on earth tones (specifically those rolling off the plow), bovine by-products, fresh mimeo-graphs, and antibiotic-infused turkey scat, I have since refined and expanded my palette to include the smell of privilege, graft, suspect sushi, and hot leaking motor oil.

Full disclosure: A blow to the head inflicted by a claustro-phobic and frankly inconsiderate Red Angus bull sometime in the 1980s temporarily knocked out my sense of smell (a deficit I first noticed the day my two-pack-a-day grandma stubbed out her Carlton 100 in the living room and rushed past me in the kitchen, reached into the oven, and removed a burning roast) and exacerbated residual impairments dating back to a high school incident involving an overdose of English Leather and the acci-dental snorting of a leaky sampler of Drakkar Noir.

Happily, I have since recovered the majority of my olfactory capacities and am prepared to apply them toward the thorough review of pine tree air fresheners, cut-rate body sprays, and a comprehensive range of scratch-n-sniff novelty items. Rather than focusing solely on prepackaged items, I will also be available to judge the aroma of new gloves, baling twine in sunshine, hot welding slag, and—for the price of airfare—the scent of Carib-bean beaches in January.

Eschewing the five-star rating system that so limited Mr. Burr, I shall instead stick to three ratings: the Double Allergan, which means my sinuses froze right up, buyer beware; the Diffident Sniff, denoting an inoffensive but unremarkable scent; and finally, the Piddly Puppy, which means I took a lungful and it smelled so good I had a little accident (see: fresh-ground coffee beans).

In 2010, Mr. Burr resigned his critic's position to become cura-tor of the world's first department of olfactory art at the Museum of Arts and Design in New York City, and still the *Times* has not called me.

I guess I'll have to strike out on my own. There is much to be smelt, and my nose is available immediately. Please submit all requests in writing, preferably in a scented envelope. Buck lure, fresh maple syrup, and brand new tractor tires go straight to the top of the pile.

BUSTED

There is that moment after the sheriff's deputy has trailed you attentively over the course of two long miles and through the second traffic circle when you resign yourself to the idea that you are about to make his acquaintance, so I wasn't that surprised when the strobes lit up and we both eased over to the shoulder.

Up to that point, it had been a lovely Sunday. I'd loaded our old plow truck (a '94 Silverado, scratched, dinged, and dented but eminently serviceable and fresh from having the brakes tuned and taillights checked) with fishing gear, a pair of kayaks, and my younger daughter's flowered bicycle, then drove north to meet the rest of the family for a day at the lake. There had been rain off and on, but not enough to dampen what became an enjoyable outing. Now I was on my way home.

I spotted the law enforcement vehicle in my rearview mirror the moment I entered the highway and had thus been driving in classic student-driver halo mode (two hands on the wheel, two miles per hour below the limit, assiduous attention devoted to all blind spots and the much-neglected fog line, signaling my turns with all the piety of a country priest). Of course driving under this sort of scrutiny puts one in a state of taut attentiveness conducive to involuntary twitches and radical overcorrection leading to a sudden inexplicable fear of yanking the wheel straight into oncoming traffic, but I kept it together, so the only thing I could figure was I was being pulled over for subpar kayak strapping.

"Sir . . ." said the deputy, now at my elbow.

Unless you're a guy on one knee and the Queen of England is tapping you on the shoulder with the flat side of a sword, anytime anyone in a uniform addresses you as "sir," you are about to receive disappointing news.

". . . are you aware . . ."

Even if it *is* the Queen of England, any sentence predicated by the phrase "are you aware" is bound to deliver heartbreak.

". . . that your registration is expired?"

Well, I wasn't expecting that.

"I had no idea," I said. Absolutely true, and absolutely unbelievable (let me state for the record that the officer did not roll his eyes, which makes him a better man than I). I am pathologically absentminded, but in matters of legality and licensure I tend to be pretty much the conscientious schoolboy. Still, I suppose I might have overlooked the blue-and-white postcard while assembling last month's bills.

"Yes sir," said the officer. "Since last July."

"Almost a *year* then," said my internal voice. "That's some professional-grade forgettin'!" (In my experience, when dealing with an officer of the law, it is best to let your internal voice do most of the talking, *internally.*)

With my outer voice, I said, "Wow." While the deputy still had no reason to believe me, I suspect my flabbergasted tone may have nudged him in that direction.

"I am going to have to write you a citation," he said. "What I'd suggest you do is register the vehicle as soon as possible. Then, if you go to court with proof of registration, the district attorney may dismiss the fine."

So now I have a court date. In some of the circles I travel, this lends me specific credibility, but I'm not going to overdo my swagger. In fact, based on previous experience I expect to argue my case on shaky knees while spitting cotton.

Oddly enough, the last time I stood within the courthouse in question it was for a drunk driving case in which I got kicked off the jury for *not* drinking. Nonetheless, I intend to throw myself at the mercy of Lady Justice, who in this case may be wearing Carhartts. The court date is a month away. Pretrial publicity is already an issue since any number of my firefighter and ambulance pals monitor the local law enforcement frequencies and are quite unprofessionally delighted with the whole deal.

Next up, a review of my rap sheet.

TRAFFIC RAP

I am fresh off an encounter with the law over the matter of that little sticker in the lower right-hand corner of my license plate being the wrong color. This has led me to attempt to recall all the times I have conversed with an officer of the law through my driver's side window.

The first time I was ever pulled over I was on my way to church. I was released with a warning (there were statutory issues concerning the height of the rear bumper on my jacked-up Plymouth Duster) but only after a steady stream of fellow parishioners had pulled around and passed us, some of them making faces that don't belong on someone headed for church.

There have been miscellaneous stops over burnt-out headlights ("padiddle!") that have faded into the mists of memory, although I do remember being detained twice within two minutes and six blocks for the same nonfunctioning taillight. I wanted to ask the second officer if he'd been listening to his radio lately, but I also wanted to go straight home so I simply showed him my fresh paperwork.

Once during a book tour I was driving an endless stretch of I-80 while speaking to a New York City publicist on my first-ever cellphone when an Iowa state patrolman pulled up behind me, then pulled around beside me, then dropped back in behind me again. "I think I have to go," I told the publicist, and sure enough the strobes came on. I was a tad shaggy in those days and had been on tour for so long that the front seat of the car looked like there had been an explosion at the fast-food-container recycling center. When the officer asked where I was headed and I told him I was on book tour, he gave me the ol' *yeah, right* squint and asked for proof. With his permission, I dug down into the trash up to my armpit and pulled out a copy of my book. He took it, looked at the photo on the dust flap, looked at me, recommended I hang up and drive, and sent me on my way.

I was once given a parking ticket by my own sister. The lead-up to that one is too long to share here, so just take my word for it and trust that justice is sometimes *willfully* blind.

I made it until my mid-thirties before I got my first actual citation, after gambling on a yellow and getting nipped by the red. A few weeks later I was driving on a county highway when I looked down and saw to my alarm that I was going seventy-two miles per hour in a fifty-five. When I looked back up, I saw flashing red and blue lights. "Sir," said the patrolman as he leaned to the window, "I clocked you at seventy-two miles per hour." "That's exactly what I had!" I said, and while that got us off on a genial good foot, it did not get me off in the legal sense. Apparently when you drive seventeen miles per hour over the limit you drive right on out of wiggle room.

Some years ago while traversing a vast stretch of darkened Oklahoma highway posted at seventy-five I noticed two weak streetlights and a cluster of buildings. I remember thinking, "I wonder if this is a speed zone," and then—as the spinning red light appeared in my rearview mirror—thinking, "I bet *he* knows." Turns out the speed limit went from seventy-five to thirty-five in the space of a flower garden. While I am loath to moan about speed traps, the fact that the officer was wearing a T-shirt, his squad was a used K-car with magnetic bubble-gum light (complete with curly cord running down to his cigarette lighter plug), and the offhand way he informed me if I paid up on the spot my record would remain clean (I did, and it did), I would like to think that one doesn't count.

OLD COP, NEW COP

This marks the third consecutive story about my recent road-side visit with a sheriff's deputy (I was driving with a profoundly lapsed registration), and this time I'd like to share the one reassuring element of the incident, and it is this: The policeman who pulled me over had gray hair and a few wrinkles.

Roughly one decade ago I was working on a project in my brother-in-law's shop. It was one-thirty a.m. before I headed for home. My route took me through a small village with one stoplight. I had recently met the woman who would become my wife and was in a state of what my brother John calls "twitterpation," which may have contributed to the fact that I came to a full stop and sat for some time before I realized the light was—and had been—green.

Shaking my head, I accelerated and pulled away. Half a block later, the village police car filled my rearview. I checked my speedometer: thirty-five in a thirty-five. No worries. But the squad followed me out of town, past the high school, past the exit to the freeway, and just as I began to accelerate for the fifty-five-mile-per-hour zone, the blue and red lights lit up.

There was a long wait as he ran my plates, then the officer exited and approached. He swept the interior of my car with his light and I cringed, because I'd been commuting and working in the shop several days straight and the car was swimming in junk and truck parts and gas station food wrappers. When he put the light on me, it wasn't much better: a dirty, unshaven goober out driving oddly after midnight.

"Good evening, sir," he said, lowering his flashlight beam just enough so that I could see him. He was a small fellow, and disturbingly young. His gun belt hung on him like he dug it out of Daddy's drawer to play dress-up. Leaning down to speak, he also tried to catch a whiff of my breath.

"Have you been drinking, sir?"

"Nope. Not for thirty-eight years."

"Well, sir, I noticed you drifting over the fog line several times."

This was flatly bullfeathers. If he had said he became suspicious when I spent five minutes camped at a green light, I'd have been down with that. But here he was plainly fishing.

"May I see your license, sir?"

With an eye toward his youth and his gun, I explained that I had to dig around some and waited for his permission. While I was digging I was thinking he was gonna love my license, which at that time featured a photo of me with frayed butt-length hair and an overgrown beard. Coulda been a membership card for the National Association of Deranged Street Prophets.

He spent a long time back there in the squad, allowing me a period of reflection. I have always believed that good cops can't be thanked enough for doing their impossible job, and as far as I know, the toddler back there running my plates was one of the good guys, but every time he spoke to me I had this urge to turn him over my knee. It occurred to me that one becomes an old coot by increments, including the first time you get stopped by a cop who looks less like an authority figure than a fresh-pressed Webelo.

Reappearing at my elbow, he handed my license through the window. "You can go," he said. Then he leaned back in the window.

"But, sir?"

"Yes?"

"Try to pay a little better attention to your driving."

"Ooookayyy . . . ," I said, turning red in the dark and wishing I had the guts to add, ". . . *Spanky.*"

The remainder of my drive was consumed with muttering.

And so, when I looked in the mirror at the approaching officer during my most recent traffic stop, I was relieved to see that gray hair. I still wasn't happy, but at least I wouldn't have to repress the whippersnapper factor. I took my medicine, and not once did I feel the urge to tell him to go finish his paper route.

COURT DATE

I am now free to drive through Chippewa County, Wisconsin.

I was recently cited ("pinched," as my father puts it) for operating my 1994 Chevrolet pickup in a manner constituting flagrant disregard for the rule of law. Specifically, I had forgotten to renew my registration.

For about a year.

The officer provided me with a citation totaling $263.50, but also provided me with an envelope I could send in to request a court date. If I registered the truck and paid a late fee in the next forty-eight hours, he said, there was a chance the county would waive the fine. First thing the following morning, I went online and paid up. Then I got a court date.

My pretrial conference was scheduled for eight-thirty on a Tuesday morning. I can report that if the justice dispensed in the Chippewa County Courthouse is as solid as the hallway bench where I awaited my fate, good people have reason to hope. One bench over, three older men awaiting jury duty were visiting. They seemed like an even-handed bunch, although their animated review of the previous evening's Brewers game didn't bode well for any defendant betraying allegiance to the Twins or Yankees.

A uniformed bailiff took my name and reviewed my paperwork, then told me I was second in line. When the assistant district attorney arrived and set up shop in the conference room I overheard him telling the bailiff that during a weekend boating trip his little dog had fallen in the lake, followed by his daughter and her boyfriend, but that all had been taken safely back on board. I hoped this meant he was in a buoyant mood.

While the driver first on the list pled his case (the bailiff shut the door, so no more eavesdropping), I made sure to put on my reading glasses in hopes that they might convey seriousness and vulnerability (I also wore a shirt with a collar), and then lectured myself over and over: *Just answer the questions, no funny stuff.* I have a pathological urge to turn everything into a joke, which in some cases has helped pay the rent, but in *court* cases can *cost* you the rent.

Even so, when I was summoned and seated, I couldn't help but critique the court date form upon which I had to check "Guilty" and pay the fine or "Not Guilty" and challenge the citation. I explained to the assistant district attorney that these two options were syntactically constrictive, and suggested adding the option of checking "Guilty but throwing myself at mercy of the court."

He received my suggestion with a polite I-didn't-really-hear-that smile, and I'm pretty sure they're not gonna change the form. Then he looked over my fresh receipt and registration, filled out a triplicate form, underlined the word "dismiss," and spun it around for my signature. "In this county we're more interested in making sure you're legal than we are in beating you up," he said. I thought this a lovely sentiment, but decided not to expand on it. I just signed, said thank you, and got outta there.

Back on the streets I've been dying to walk around all seasoned-like, squinting and saying out of the corner of my mouth, "I beat the rap," but A) I didn't so much beat the rap as meekly beg out of it, and B) that's a tad cocky and a guy doesn't want to find his karma account overdrawn. Plus, one week after I renewed last year's lapsed registration, the postcard for next year's registration arrived, so I am already at risk for relapse.

Prolly—as those of us raised up in Chippewa County like to say—gonna wanna git right on'nat.

DRIVERLESS CARS

This morning while moving the chicken tractor without aid of GPS, I listened as a man on the radio talked about the coming wave of driverless cars. Actually, he kept talking about this "sort of" wave of driverless cars and these "sort of" ethical issues that will "sort of" confront automakers. I have recently stated in public that the modifiers "sort of" and "kind of" (as in, "It was a sort of a massacre, followed by kind of an inferno") have become the public radio equivalent of "like" and "y'know." I also then hastened to add that as a guy who regularly catches myself saying all four (sometimes in a single sentence) I have no room to talk, and furthermore this is the type of observation that arrives wrapped in a whiff of my own creeping codgerism (another recurring affliction that seems to compound interest daily), which I daily resolve to tamp down, and if not tamp, temper.

I have now reviewed where the following paragraph began and where it wound up, and clearly my mind is its own sort of driverless car.

Back on task: The man on the radio caught my attention because driverless cars are interesting and incoming, but also because I recently spent time teaching a fifteen-year-old how to operate a stick shift and I have the neck sprains to prove it. We are midway through the driver licensing process for this member of the family, and there is the usual mix of pride, hope, and abject fear for everyone involved. So far so good. A little herky-jerky getting out of first gear, sure, but getting better.

The man in the interview said these days the roads are filled with drivers who have never learned to operate a stick shift. I am determined that my kid will not be one of these, but in fact, fewer young people are driving, *period,* let alone running a clutch, so it could be my pride and efforts are misplaced. After all, we have quite happily turned ourselves over to our phones—I trust we'll be just as pleased to surrender the steering wheels of our cars in order that we might devote more time to our phones.

More interesting to me than the technology aspects of the interview were the ethical issues being raised: If a driverless car detects another vehicle speeding toward it from the rear and must decide between swerving into a crowded sidewalk or taking the hit, what will its circuits choose? At this point the engineers are sitting down with philosophers and ethicists. As with many things, it isn't the technology that's tough, it's the transition. The "human-machine interface," as the driverless car folks put it.

If this creeping codger has learned one thing in the past twenty years it is that scoffing something is not the same as stopping something. Barring an apocalyptic event (in which case the resale on a chicken tractor may exceed that of a driverless car) my children will one day be merging with these vehicles in both the cultural and on-ramp senses.

I'm not sure it will be such a big deal. One of the reasons I am so content to be puttering around with my chickens in the backyard is because I have only recently emerged from a sustained stretch in which I spent more time on the road than at home or at rest, and based on my observations—confirmed by the ridiculous reflexive urge to check my own phone every few minutes—a profound percentage of the cars out there are *already* driverless.

F. SCOTT FITZGERALD TEST

I hope you weren't hiding out back behind the corn crib the other evening when I strolled out to close the chicken coop, because if you were, and you were wearing night vision goggles, then you saw me fail the F. Scott Fitzgerald test. (You also heard language that would get me banned from the Navy—but let's focus on one character deficit at a time.)

The thing is, I knew the tree was out there, because halfway across the yard in the dark I made a mental note of it. It had grown to block the sun from reaching the photovoltaic panels on our granary, so when some fellows from a tree service came to trim a few limbs overhanging our house and offered to drop the sunblocker for no charge, I gave them the go-ahead. Some people would have chunked it up into firewood immediately, but those people are smug overachievers. In the interest of humility I left it lying across a corner of the yard for three weeks.

But I hadn't forgotten it. And so it was, as I crossed the yard in overcast darkness devoid of moon or starlight, I thought, *I don't want to slam my shins into that prostrate tree,* so I fished my smartphone out of my pocket, intending to punch up a flashlight app. As I swiped around searching for it, rather than stop, I kept walking while staring down at the screen in that hunched form of ambulation that has taken less than a generation to seep into the human genome and threatens to reverse the evolutionary chart, at least as it pertains to posture. Just as I located and tapped the digital flashlight, I slammed my shins full force into that prostrate tree.

The jokes about dumb people with smart phones really write themselves, and I'll leave you to it. What really needs examination is my attention span, which can apparently be measured only with an atomic micrometer. How is it that a person can spot trouble ahead, take action to avoid it, but barge right on into it anyway?

The most concrete evidence (beyond my scored and purpled shins, which are quite literally "barked") of my having real issues in this area is documented by my brown pole barn. I have two pole barns. They're nothing fancy, not insulated or heated or anything like that, but they do have concrete floors and they don't leak much, and two-thirds of the sliding doors actually slide—although the one screeches like a scalded owl—and overall the corrugated tin is in pretty good shape, and a guy would like to keep it that way. So as I backed the tractor out of the brown shed on a mission to cut back the burdock encroaching its borders, I made a mental note to remember that in addition to the rear-mounted brush hog, I must remain aware of the front-mounted loader. In the process of completing that thought—and while sitting with my head swiveled back to admire how the brush hog was annihilating the burdock—I swung the front end of the tractor around and punched the loader right through the pole barn wall. Honestly, *milliseconds* had passed since I reminded myself *not to do that.*

F. Scott Fitzgerald once wrote, "The test of a first-rate intelligence is the ability to hold two opposing ideas in mind at the same time and still retain the ability to function." While contemplating the perforated tin and thanking my lucky stars that I got 'er shut down before I ripped the shed open like a tin of split kippers, it struck me that my skull is apparently unable to simultaneously contain the concept of a rear-mounted mower and a front-end loader without sticking one of them where it does not belong (or cohabitate the ideas that *the tree will hurt* and *the tree is RIGHT THERE*), and this would seem to bode ill for my next shot at the Mensa tryouts.

Looking at my shins right now, I am reminded of cheese grat-ers and spoiled plums. But at least that will fade. Not so every time I go down to the shed for a fence post or a hog panel and face that triangulate gash. I believe it is good and bracing—now and then—to confront your own mortality; I wish I could say I felt the same about confronting my own mentality.

GOTTA GO WORK OUT

Well, I gotta go work out. I have gone just over two weeks without official exercise. I took the break to accommodate a family trip, which was well worth it in the memory department but a tad anemic in the exercise department. There was some minor hiking, a day of whitewater rafting, one day spent chaperoning an eight-year-old on repeat rides of an Alpine slide in the Rocky Mountains (she giggled, I turned green), and one breathless session of carrying luggage and groceries up three flights of stairs at 9,600 feet, but there was also a stretch of simply sitting in a boat fishing, several thousand miles locked in a van, and more than a little untoward late-night snacking.

Prior to the trip I'd been a regular at a local workout session, averaging five days a week. I was also logging four to six miles per day at my treadmill desk, where I find I hit peak production at 2.2 miles per hour. I've written about the treadmill desk in the past, but I am always hesitant to mention it, as it is the sort of device that is difficult to explain to the loggers, farmers, and Marines in the family.

But the truth hurts, and the painful fact in this case is I have reached that point in my physical life where one focuses more on maintenance than excellence. And if that means standing in a circle with a few friends and neighbors doing jumping jacks ("Be light on your feet!" the trainer cheers, and I wonder what that feels like), well, where's my leotard? (In fact, I wear a pair of loose shorts purchased on clearance from a large box store.) (They are the color of an underripe avocado marinated in irradiated lime juice.) (They are also a source of great social discomfort for my children.) (Thus: perfect.) (I also find that the yellow-greenish shorts distract the attention of anyone who might otherwise be studying my form during our various abdominal-based contortions, in particular a medieval little number I can only describe as recumbent four-stage toe-touchers: Imagine a capsized turtle pawing blindly at an army of ankle-biting mosquitos.)

My first day back was actually yesterday. We started out easy with some high knee-lifts and pretend jump roping (again, tough to broach with the loggers), then segued into upper-body twists and jogging in place, which is all just pretext to the dreaded abdominals segment, a cruel fantasy predicated on the idea that one actually has abdominals. In fact the session went better than anticipated. Apparently inactivity and bad snacking can be countered if performed at high altitude. The only drastic sign of deterioration occurred toward the end of the session, when I attempted a side plank and within seconds found myself trembling, wavering, and eventually lurching in a manner that eludes specific description but I think could be conveyed via seismograph.

Also, this morning I am sore in some critical areas, not the least of which upon I sit. ("Walk it off!" my machinist brother-in-law would say, to which I dare not reply, "On my special treadmill desk?") So, back on the horse. Or at least mime jump roping. Today being washday, I will wear my regular old gray shorts. I'm not sure how that will affect my performance, but I expect the public in general will be grateful.

I am eager to regain my peak form. It won't take long. The bar is low; I don't have far to go.

NOT A LOGGER

I frequently invoke the logging profession as a means of calibrating my own self-perception, particularly when I am tempted to portray myself as a bit of a rough-and-tumble fellow from the back forty, when in truth the closest I come to processing forest products—firewood excepted—is that moment when I break out a fresh ream of paper for my laser printer.

That said, I was raised in a logging family. I can distinguish between a cant hook and a peavey, I know bar oil is not intended for use in cocktails, and given twice as much time as my brother, I can sharpen a saw chain half as well (the key is to trim those rakers—just enough, not too much). I know a forwarder from a skidder from a feller buncher, my great-grandfather was a "river rat," and I understand that the term "widow maker" (used to describe a tree that is hung up or positioned in such a way that it poses an extreme threat to the person felling it) is not strictly euphemistic. My cousin lost her first husband in a logging accident. I was there the day a white pine log rolled over and snapped my uncle's arm. My logger brother's profession landed him in intensive care twice—once with a split skull. And as a rural first responder, I can recall all too vividly the fatal logging accidents I've "worked," and how it felt—especially in the case when I was the first on scene—to approach the fallen tree, knowing all too well what I was about to see.

It was against this background that I raised the chainsaw last week and—noticing the eye-level limb I was about to trim was bent beneath the weight of another fallen limb—paused. While I am no lumberjack, based on background (and my brother's skull) I could predict that once the limb was severed, the butt end would whip around in the manner of a swung baseball bat. Eyeballing the distance from the limb to my, well, *eyeball,* I backed off and began my cut from a position and angle well clear of the potential radius of the swing. As the saw teeth bit into the wood, I felt an amateur's unearned pride in having known enough to make this preemptive professional move.

Having never been kicked in the face by an actual mule, I can't say what I felt next would in any way compare. The example is perhaps a tad dramatic and may undersell the mule. In fact, the swiftness of it really didn't allow for a lot of comparative analysis. Rather than following the radial path of a swung bat, the branch sprang straight, driving the sawn end directly into my cheekbone in the manner of a pool cue smacking a cue ball. I managed to safely shut down the saw, then lurched about clutching my visage while uttering untoward phrases we shall politely blame on "concussion effects."

The next morning, when my cheekbone had scabbed over and the area below my left eye had begun its transition through the grimmer shades of the rainbow, I studied the results in the mirror and thanked my lucky spinning stars for the safety glasses I had donned just before starting the saw.

In the days that followed, I found myself having to explain my redecorated face to friends and strangers alike. For humor's sake, I invoked everything from human billiards to three seconds in the ring with Rhonda Rousey. I also heard a lot of grim stories reinforcing my dumb luck. In general it has been resolved: As a logger, I make a pretty good typist, and should focus mostly on handling only those trees available in the form of office supplies.

NO BETTER ANGEL

As I paused the van beside the corn crib with the front bumper pointed toward the back forty, my better angel whispered, "You know, that might not be the best idea."

"You'll be fine," said my lazy angel, rolling his eyes.

Earlier this fall I noticed the tires on our thirteen-year-old van had about as much tread as I have hair on my head. After consulting the budget and the calendar and cross-referencing this information with the fact that we had a fresh pair of snow tires in the garage, we decided to eke out a few more miles and postpone the tire expenditure until the next fiscal year.

Now I had ridden those bald tires to town and back on some errands. As I pulled into the yard I remembered that I intended to haul some items out to a deer blind that afternoon. It was cold outside, and the van was toasty warm. "You should take the plow truck," said my better angel. "It has four-wheel drive."

"The van is toasty warm," said my lazy angel. "Isn't it nice?"

The lazy angel is so much easier to get along with. He just wants me to be happy. And comfy. And besides, although the blind was deep into the property, a mown two-track ran all the way out there.

"So warm," said the lazy angel, and off I went.

I made it to the blind no problem, but after turning for home the treadless tires spun out on a greasy patch of mud. I rocked back and forth, but there was more back than forth, and soon not only was I stuck, my rear bumper was wedged against a tree, so even back wasn't an option. Afoot, I headed for home.

When I called my neighbor Denny twenty minutes later, I was out of breath from all the hiking (and possibly the cussing). Denny is the kind of neighbor who delights in this sort of boneheaded escapade, but he is also the kind of neighbor who drops everything to help, whether you deserve it or not, so he's entitled to his chuckle. With Denny in the plow truck we pulled the van free easily.

Fast-forward to the following evening. I have to retrieve a deer from the woods. Night has already fallen by the time I go down to the pole barn to start the ATV. It cranks and cranks but won't start—which is odd, because it started fine just two days ago. Finally the battery begins to fade. I'll take the tractor, I think. When I turn that key, the starter makes clicking noises then falls silent. What are the odds, I think, and depart for the plow truck, which is still parked where Denny left it. When I twist the key all the gauges light up—the battery is fine—but the starter won't engage. At this point I wonder if some sort of malevolent magnetic field is in play. My wife and daughters are gone with the car, so I am now down to one functional vehicle . . . the van. I use it to jump the tractor but that battery is so shot it won't take a charge. I try the ATV again. The starter gives a few sad spins and fades. Almost as an afterthought, I unscrew the gas cap and direct my headlamp within. Bone-dry. I gas it up, do some quick smartphone research on how to jump-start an ATV with a car battery, and in short order it's putt-putting beautifully.

The moral of the story is not clear. But: I knew those tires were bald; the truck starter was acting up last winter; that tractor battery needed a jump the last two times I ran it; and as far as the gasless ATV, well, stupid never runs empty. As I drove into the darkened woods to finally fetch the deer, I took a shot at calculating the hours lost and blood pressure points blown thanks to my lazy angel. "Oh, don't do math," he said. "Math is hard."

My better angel said nothing, knowing I never listen anyway.

PITCHING A FIT

I recently pitched a little fit.

Perhaps the phrase requires some fine-tuning: The fit was "little" in that it didn't last long. The *amplitude,* however, well, that was a different story. If I had been hooked up to the *Fit-Pitcher 3000,* I'd have scorched the contacts, bent the needle, and we'd be hunting new fuses.

I would also like to pass this off as an isolated incident, an aberration surprising everyone involved, including myself. The problem is, myself was not surprised. Myself has seen this kind of behavior before.

And perhaps that is the only redeeming element of this tale: Rather than endangering the community around me, these rages are directed at only one person: the guy whose laminated face stares dumbly out from my driver's license. He is a constant source of deep frustration. He dithers. He procrastinates. He trudges all the way down to the pole barn and trudges all the way back upstairs to where he's removing the air conditioner only to realize the wrench he fetched was an $11/16$, not a $5/8$. He is, in short, a real teeth-grinding disappointment.

In my day-to-day interactions with the world, I comport myself with reliable restraint. In fact, I have been told by those who love me that I am overly laid-back in this respect and get run over in the process, but I have no appetite for fighting. Even when cut off in traffic I opt for the sardonic aside over cursing and flying the bird. During blood pressure–busting customer service phone calls I choose dispassion over harangue.

But when it is just myself? I recently made it six miles down the road to a band gig only to realize I had left the box of CDs behind—*the box of CDs I placed directly in front of the door so I wouldn't forget them and as a result had to STEP OVER THEM UPWARDS OF FIVE TIMES IN THE PROCESS OF FORGETTING THEM*—and, well, let's just say I laid some spittle on the windshield and (in the style of the late Chris Farley) may have hit myself right in my own head. After disappointing myself on behalf of myself in another incident some years ago, I Frisbee-flung and broke the top to a perfectly good papasan chair after becoming angry with myself for punching a metal file box after becoming angry with myself for . . . for . . . well, I don't remember, because I was so embarrassed by the whole papasan thing. I repented that one for years to come, shamed every time I sat in the papasan and had to look at the part where the bamboo was held together with duct tape.

As with most shameful bad habits, I try to hide this behavior, and in most cases succeed. (There was the time my wife entered my writing room undetected and caught me in the act of giving myself a real good high-decibel cussing—upon reflection, she didn't intervene quickly and may have been happy to stand there and let me let myself have it.) (This incident was only one notch less embarrassing than the time she caught me singing the chorus of Supertramp's "Give a Little Bit" at the top of my lungs.) But still, I carry the shame. We wonder, sometimes, if we are the only ones who act this way.

This past month I attended a literary event of medium-to-high order and encountered an acquaintance I have long admired for his character, tenacity, and commitment to good. He appeared a tad rattled. In the process of conversation he revealed that he had just emerged from a solo session in his office involving a misplaced deadline and a malfunctioning printer. Finally, after some discussion, he revealed (Okay, I egged him on until he admitted) that the episode culminated in his standing alone in the room and screaming at himself for being such a [REDACTED] [REDACTED] *IDIOT!*

I felt so bad for him, I couldn't help giggling out loud.

Myself has seen this kind of behavior before.

MUDDED UP

During the early December thaw we were preparing for a family trip (which is to say roaring around trying to cram a week's worth of to-dos into a single afternoon) when I found myself needing to move several boxes of books and some band gear from my van into my office. The office is in a small room above our garage, and because the garage is built into a hill, my office door—which opens to the rear of the building—is set just a few stair steps above ground level. This allows me to back the van right up to the door for loading and unloading.

The path to the office door isn't paved. It's simply twin tire paths worn into the grass. As I lined up the path in my rearview mirror, it struck me that the thaw had left things feeling very springlike, right up to and including a certain squishiness to the earth when I walked out to water the chickens earlier. There was that fleeting moment when I wondered if leaving the paved driveway was a bad idea, but then impatience took over (it is never really off duty) and I dropped the transmission into reverse and hit the gas.

I made it to the office door no problem.

Two hours later I finished up and jumped into the van to drive it down to the house for reloading. We were now T-minus one hour to departure.

I made it about six feet when the front wheels spun out. I got that little sub–liver level adrenaline squirt you get when you think maybe there's gonna be a problem, the chemical manifestation of *uh-oh!* But then I rocked 'er back two feet and got another run at it. Made it about four feet, then spun out. This went on for about four cycles—gain four feet, give up two.

And then the tires spun again, but this time when I tried reverse the van moved nary a millimeter. Back and forth I tried; Drive, Reverse, Drive, Reverse. Nothing. I even did that deal where you use the steering wheel to kinda lever yourself up from the seat, as if lightening your butt is gonna somehow help (the gravitational equivalent of blowing on your own sail). I also leaned forward intently, drawing on some instinctive belief that I could create momentum with the tilt of my torso.

Nothing. Just the muffled *whizzz!* of tires fruitlessly spinning.

There are times when a guy screams into the windshield. There are times when a guy bangs his fists on the steering wheel like a three-year-old throwing a tantrum because he dropped his lollipop. And then there are times—despite all previous history of engaging in the behavior just cited—when a guy thinks of the family packing in the house downhill, realizes he has one chance to get this right, and goes into laser focus mode.

I headed straight for the house. Briefed my wife on the situation. "I won't ask *why*," she said, which of course is just another way of asking *why.* "I'm going to need you to drive," I said (with a certain meekness of tone), and then jumped into a pair of work pants and a hoodie given me by my alma mater, who at moments like this probably wish I wouldn't advertise. I found the tow strap behind the seat of the four-wheel-drive plow truck, right where it was supposed to be, and gave up a prayer of thanks. I decided I didn't want to risk burying the four-wheel-drive pickup and instead went right for the four-wheel-drive tractor. At the last minute I traded the tow strap for a logging chain, a gamble predicated on my locating the actual tow loops on the van (upon which sighting I offered up another thank-you) and the configuration of the log chain hooks. Crawling around under there I got soaked and muddy and was glad I had taken the time to change—usually I'd have shortcutted my way into unforgivable laundry.

And then, with my wife at the wheel, I pulled the van out nice and easy, first try.

It's funnier when things go all wrong, I know. But now and then, things go right, even for us stumblebums. And as I looked at those ruts in the lawn, I smiled. Sometimes it's good to pull a bonehead move, if only for the glory of getting out of it.

I did not run this observational nugget past my wife.

FRIENDS AND RELATIONS

KEEP YOUR HEAD WARM

Once upon a Santa Claus season my mother sewed my grandfather a soft red cap with a tassel on top. Grandpa had requested the gift to keep his bald head warm at night, and when he unwrapped and donned it while sitting in his recliner we kids were tickled to see him looking just like the fellow who tore open the shutters and threw up the sash in the *'Twas the Night before Christmas* picture book we'd read. As far as I know Grandpa wore that nightcap to bed every cold-air evening for the rest of his life.

Grandpa was always touchy about his bald head. Not in a self-conscious way—he was the first to appreciate a good hair-loss joke—but rather in a literal sense. He starched and wore his mesh golfer caps with the crown set absurdly high so none of the material came in contact with his scalp, and although he'd cuddle a grandchild, if it started pawing at—or worse, drooling on—his pate, he'd dangle the youngster at arm's length until rescue arrived. And should he strike his barren bean on a solid object—say, an open kitchen cupboard door—there would immediately commence a desperate jig in which he bounced around the kitchen alternately clutching his head and daintily dabbing with his fingertips to check for blood, all the while repeating his two grandchildren-safe cuss words: "Mustard and custard and mustard and custard!"

This from a man who survived the sands of Iwo Jima.

In high school my hair was thick and grand. (Or at least I thought so: if mirrors were rented by the hour I'd have been running a steady deficit.) Through college I leveraged this follicular abundance to achieve hairstyles considered hip for only about forty-five seconds in the mid-1980s, and then only in poorly lit New Wave music videos. For most of the 1990s I let it grow long and wore it without fuss. By the millennium I experienced my first scalp sunburn (a sensation I equated to a combination of hives and paranormal possession), and then came the winter evening when I lay abed in our drafty old farmhouse and felt my denuded dome slowly assume the state of a chilled honeydew melon.

I thought of Grandpa.

It is one thing when we see ourselves becoming our parents, quite another when we see ourselves becoming our grandparents. That night, for the first time not counting campouts, I drifted off to sleep beneath headgear.

Over summer one fools oneself into feeling youthful and resumes snoozing in a state of doff. But last night when I settled into the mattress only to feel the autumnal chill seeping through the plaster and into my cranium, I thought of Grandpa again, then jumped up and dug around in the closet for my nightcap. Mine isn't storybook stylish, it's just an old stocking cap with a missing tassel. It was knit by a relative and given to my brother John for Christmas when we were kids. I don't know how I came to possess it, but I wish you wouldn't tell John, mainly because he still has his hair and thus deserves no quarter. Over the decades the cap has become stretched and misshapen, which is a good thing because my head is the circumference of a prize-winning gourd and the last thing you want is a tight nightcap. You wake up cross-eyed, with sweaty ears and yarn prints pressed into your forehead.

Although he died before I lost my hair, I was fortunate to know Grandpa well into my adulthood and thus had a chance to observe his character beyond the vantage point of Christmas morning. He was a good man, and I would do well to be more like him. He taught me to fish. He taught me to read Plato. He taught me that the key to every successful hunting trip was good sandwiches. And above all else? Keep your head warm.

TIO MIGUEL

I have never been a smoker. I maintain those butts I scrounged out of the ashtray of our old Ford Falcon station wagon when I was nine don't count, because they were impossible to keep lit. Nor do I count the repulsive torpedo I fired up in my role as "Speed" in the Chippewa Valley Theater Guild's 1992 production of *The Odd Couple*. That was stage smoking: no inhaling, and four nights only. For rehearsal, I filched my grandma's Carlton 100s. Finally, as a guy who has spent a fair amount of time in the company of musicians and poets, I have had plenty of secondhand exposure to what Grandpa referred to as the ol' wacky tobacky, but again, I've never sparked up myself.

I report this not to claim any sort of righteousness, but rather to set a point of reference for the one time I did—intentionally—have a smoke.

I grew up on your classic Wisconsin farm. White house, red barn, black and white cows in a green field. My brother-in-law Marcelino grew up in a Panamanian barrio. No backyard, just chickens scratching in dirt. He was baseball crazy and earned a tryout with the Baltimore Orioles. Today one of his childhood friends from the old neighborhood is a major leagues millionaire, but Marcelino says he knew ten minutes into his tryout that he wasn't going to make the cut. Thanks to an exchange program, he was able to enroll in classes at a state technical college, and now he does computer drafting for a company in a small Wisconsin town.

Marcelino married my wife's sister, and when their first baby—a boy—came in August, Marcelino was as proud as any papa would be. When they visited after the boy was born, I shook Marcelino's hand and thumped him on the back and congratulated him, whereupon he produced two big honking cigars. "We will smoke!" he said, and I saw such joy in his face I knew my reservations were irrelevant. He also had with him a fresh bag of Venezuelan coffee beans. I ground a batch, threw a thermos of the brew in a backpack, and then the two of us climbed into my old pickup truck and drove a few miles into the country to this forty-acre patch I know. We hiked in, and then on a hill thick with aspen and oak, Marcelino held the match while I puffed like some kid behind the barn. When both cigars were burning, we raised them and smiled, and I said, "To your son . . . to your family."

We smoked for an hour. It was September. The acorns were loosening, and every time the breeze blew, they fell like hard rain, smacking *spat, spat, spat* on last year's dead leaves. We talked about Marcelino's Panamanian childhood, the family he left behind, and the fear and joy of bringing a child into a world that seems to be moving faster and faster and fracturing into smaller and smaller pieces. It's an old tune. Every generation sings a reprise.

The smoke mixed deliciously with the coffee, and as the ash drew nearer to my knuckles, I began to feel it pretty good. I stood to clear my head, and nearly tipped over. The caffeine and nicotine had me buzzing like a cheap rheostat, and I could tell I was gonna go real light on supper.

But I don't regret that cigar. When it was time to stub out, we had reached no conclusions except that perhaps the best thing a man can do for his children is identify his vulnerabilities and plot accordingly. The last puff of smoke caught in the breeze and drifted to the trees. "Now you are Tio Miguel," said Marcelino. *Uncle Mike.* That made me feel good. We shook hands like brothers, then walked back to the truck.

I stepped carefully, as I could feel the world spinning.

JED CALLING

I was talking to my brother Jed on the phone last night. He was calling from his combine cab. I could hear the engine idling in the background. It was dark out, and I could imagine him, an hour north of me, out there in the middle of a Chippewa County cornfield, visible only as white lights in black space.

He had called me for advice, which right out of the gate places his judgment into question; I come from a family of eminently practical people, most of them equipped to perform fundamental functions along the lines of heavy machinery operation, projects involving electricity (on purpose), the design and production of roads and basements and cell phone parts and grain, military service, and so on. Whereas I peddle words and compose three-chord songs with soft hands. Cripes. Half my firewood this year was split and stacked by my mother-in-law and teenaged daughter—I am nobody's sturdy example. On the other hand, I have taken a wrong turn or two over time, and can sometimes provide guidance based on the resulting dents.

So there we were, my real farmer brother and writer me, separated, depending on how you look at it, by forty miles or the bounce of a satellite, each with a phone pressed to our respective ears. One of the great pleasures of speaking with my brother Jed is that he never really started talking until he was in high school, at which point I was already off the farm and into dressing like Prince (this reminds me that in some respects I have gotten my life back on track—blessed are those who left to Prince what was best left to Prince). So even as Jed and I move solidly through middle age it is still a fun surprise to hear him string a sentence together.

The topic of discussion the other evening is not mine to share, although I can say it was neither prurient nor dramatic and in fact had to do with basic self-employment strategies. In the end, I was able to supply a shaky 25 percent of the information he needed, definitely a win considering the source.

For me the true joy was in the ease and humor of the conversation. My brother has faced things I cannot imagine—the loss of a wife and child among them—so it is always good to hear him speaking in the easy goofball tones we favor when our hearts are unburdened. Furthermore, while we are not of one mind on all things, the way our voices mirror each other helps me remember that be there differences, we are still bound by blood, any rough joints morticed by a clodhopper sense of humor. Once I called him late at night when I was on book tour. Back in those days, he was driving a log truck. He was somewhere up north with a load of pulp, I was southbound through Illinois, my vehicle loaded down with books in boxes. "We're both just out here haulin' trees," I said, and when his chuckle came through the earpiece my heart swelled right up into my throat.

Finally—that night, and again last night—one of us said, "Yah, well," which meant we were easing into the hanging up, and when we did, I went back to my work and he went back to his, and it was good to think of him out there, revving up that combine as I clicked at my keyboard, somewhere up above us the satellites circling until we are drawn to speak again.

❧

CLASS REUNION

I am pleased to report that attendance for the recent reunion of the New Auburn High School Class of 1983 came in at over 50 percent, which is to say there are an even dozen of us populating the group photos now riding around in our respective cell phones, a technological development the kindergarten version of us certainly never anticipated as we beamed from our monochromatic wallet prints.

I'll limit myself in recounting the evening's festivities in part because other people's class reunion memories are like other people's vacation photos: you can smile through the first two or three out of politeness, but at some point you don't know the players involved and are therefore not emotionally invested and five minutes in you're edging toward an open fifth floor window or fighting the urge to claw madly at the nearest fire alarm.

At thirty years the memories are beginning to take on an amber hue, although once the recollections get rolling, and the stories start spilling one after another, there is the invigoration of laughter and rediscovery all leading to the inevitable moment when you shake your head and simply can't believe it all happened so long ago so *quickly*. It's an inborn human trait, our bafflement and fascination with the passage of time, and you don't have to wait three decades to feel it. Just last week my first grader was wistfully reminiscing about the halcyon days of pre-K, a time as distant to her as my memories of SkyLab and a full head of hair.

It was good to see everyone, even Greg H., who when bored with trigonometry used to chase me out of the high school math room and down the hall while brandishing the wooden leg of a dismantled chair. We've been friends since before kindergarten, when he introduced himself by hitting me in the head with a rock. It takes time to work through these things, and I still tend to be a little twitchy in his presence. At the reunion he sat across the table from me. The first time he reached for his steak knife I nearly threw my back out resisting the urge to sprint screaming into the parking lot.

As far as our classmates unable to attend, we pieced together what we knew, and what we last heard, and thus they were present too. The bulk of us spent every one of our thirteen school years—kindergarten through graduation—in the same class. You do that amount of time in proximity, you develop familial-level connections that survive all intervening time and change.

The highlight of the evening came when the waitress delivered menus printed in a font so large that we were able to read them without our recently acquired reading glasses. A shame, perhaps, because how entertaining it would have been to watch an entire table of people perform the self-pat-down dance that becomes so familiar once the eyeballs go. Someone mimed the pat-down, and the chuckle that went around the table reflected our ability to grin in the face of our own deterioration.

One of our absent classmates had arranged to finance a few rounds of drinks, so after our meal, we moved to the bar. When the bartender kindly asked us what kind of music we'd prefer on the jukebox, our immediate requests included Duran Duran, Men at Work, and Survivor, but in the end we decided it might be most appropriate to just serve up Springsteen's "Glory Days" on a continuous loop.

We only know the life we have lived. People who go to large schools in big cities forge long-lasting friendships too. But as I observed us in the mirror of the roughneck bar, showing our age, and feeling our age, and laughing agelessly in the face of it, the thought that occurred to me was *Am I ever glad I wound up being one of this bunch.*

At some point in the evening, our classmate Renee arrived, pushing attendance from an even dozen to thirteen.

It felt like a lucky number.

FIRST RESPONDERS

I'd never set foot in this fire hall before, but I knew it by heart: The homemade Maltese cross on the wall, the shelf of softball and water fight trophies, a scattering of vintage helmets and antique fire extinguishers, the canvas-smoky smell of dried hose and bunker jackets, and of course the red fire trucks sitting still and silent in the adjacent bay.

Once every two years, emergency first responders and EMTs are required to enroll in a "refresher" course, the purpose of which is to update and test those skills required in order to maintain licensure. The classes generally take place over the course of a month of weeknights and weekends. When time on the road precludes my attending the course provided by my own department, I have to hunt up a substitute, and thus it was that last Saturday morning I found myself in another town's fire hall surrounded by people I mostly—with the exception of a few faces—didn't know.

But I felt like I was among old friends. Our clothing ran to T-shirts, satin bar jackets, and camo caps, and pagers were the number one fashion accessory. The between-session conversations were the usual mix of good-natured ribbing and small-town updates. My favorite story of the day was the one of which I caught nothing but the punchline: ". . . and he polished it off with a bottle'a Boone's Farm!"

Half the fun there was filling in the blanks.

As we rehearsed the latest CPR techniques the room filled with the aroma of the crockpot potluck that would be our lunch:

baked beans, hot dogs, and barbecue. It is the nature of the business that no one in the room will give a second thought to discussing death while tucking into a second helping of sloppy joe.

At one point some joker dressed a CPR mannequin in a cap and sunglasses, propped it up in a chair, and waited for the instructor to spot it. It's an old trick but always worth a double take and a group guffaw. The rare serious moment came when we broke into groups to practice infant CPR on the doll-like mannequins. No matter how seasoned you might be, no one wants to face that call. Perhaps the most surreal moment of the day came at the conclusion of CPR and defibrillation training, when the instructor said, "Be sure to tear out the lungs and rip off the faces." A passerby unaware she was telling us how to prepare the mannequins for disinfecting might have called the SWAT team.

One of the elements of firefighting and EMS service I most cherish is how each of us comes through the door with our own diverse backgrounds and interests—sometimes with little or no overlap, and in some cases outright opposition—and yet within the context of emergencies we all speak a similar language and share a common history. We can speak in esoteric acronymns and slang ("S.A.M.P.L.E.," "scoop-n-scoot," "B.S.I.," "frequent flyer") and know exactly what someone otherwise wholly unlike ourselves is trying to convey. Should we find ourselves at the side of the road beside a wrecked car, we may not know each other's names, but we will know what to do, and do it together.

It was a sunny spring Saturday in the small town. During one break we enjoyed homemade rhubarb crisp with fire hall doors open. Outside I could hear lawn mowers and see people coming and going. Back in the dispatch center, the scanner chirped now and then, a reminder of why we were here. There were a lot of things to do on a day like this. I was perfectly happy to spend it with familiar strangers.

MY FRIEND JAIME

It was two a.m. when my friend Jaime dropped me off at my house and continued home to his own. I should let you know that although his name is pronounced "Jay-mee," the "i" is and has always been intended to precede the "m" despite how many times it has appeared otherwise, including in the credits of many albums he has helped create.

That is how we met, in fact: in the course of recording music. I was in a local coffee shop and had asked a musician friend to recommend a recording engineer. He pointed to the barista artfully frothing a macchiato, and thus I was introduced to Jaime. Over the course of the seven years since, we've recorded and produced two music albums, one live humor album, four audiobooks, several years' worth of radio show monologues, and a stewpot of digitized miscellany.

The recording studio is a fine place to forge and fine-tune a friendship. Especially when most times it's only the two of you, and you're paying by the hour. You learn to work lean—no formalities, no circular talk, no ego tending, just *yep, nope,* and *next.* But then of course there are breaks and late-night food runs, and during those times you slowly discover each other's character, interests, and vulnerabilities.

And then one day you realize you have a fine version of friendship. I say "version" with intent, because it is not one of those inextricably entwined friendships. Our time together rarely includes family or even other friends. When there is no work to be done, we go weeks or months without contact. We are not, by broad definition, "close." And yet because so much of our time together has been accumulated in close quarters at all hours, we at some point shed all formality and settled into the ease of simple human interaction. In light of the subtexts, politics, and politenesses involved in so many other relationships (and even other friendships), this is a rare and cherished gift.

Plus Jaime's a road dog. Say you have to make the afternoon run from Fall Creek, Wisconsin, to Woodstock, Illinois, in time to do load-in and sound check for an eight p.m. one-man show, then get back to Fall Creek by morning for chicken chores. Say you're already short on sleep. Say you're also on deadline for a piece of work due the following morning and you need someone to drive while you type.

This is when you call a friend like Jaime.

In addition to his studio work, Jaime lives with and is caretaker for his father, so he said he'd have to check for backup. This is another beauty of these lean, spare friendships: You don't have to frame your request or couch it in apology, you just lay it out there knowing if the answer is "yes," he'll say so, but that he's also the kind of friend you can trust to say "no" with neither party being charged any freight. In this case it was yes, and we hit the road.

We did talk some catch-up for the first hour. We talked walleye fishing and philosophy, we talked recording studio chatter, we complained about things only friends can complain about without seeming whiny, and we talked politics, because Jaime is one of those friends you can talk politics with and hope to learn something—as opposed to playing binary rhetorical ping-pong.

And then Jaime stuck his earbuds into an audiobook, and I got to work. The miles unspooled. We loaded in, I did the show, we loaded out. We headed back north, spelling each other at the wheel. And somewhere around three a.m., sixteen hours after we'd left, we were back.

"See y'later," said Jaime.

"See y'later," I said.

Friends. Working lean.

GONE FISHING

If all goes according to plan, by the time you read this I will be poised for a journey to a foreign nation and hoping for a safe return—although I take nothing for granted, and if I wind up on the wrong side of the border in any sense, please notify the embassy and tell anyone who will listen it was a good run.

I mean: Canada, but you never know.

Among my failures as a father, I have flopped on the fishing front. Not completely, not utterly—my younger daughter and I have been fishing twice this year, thanks to some friends with a dock, and there have been a few other piscatory forays with my elder daughter in previous years—but I have certainly not maintained the pace of my ancestors (my Grandma Perry included; she loved to fish, and we grandchildren still mimic the way she held the reel handle between her thumb and third finger, thus freeing up the index and middle fingers for the ever-present, ever-smoldering Carlton 100).

This trip—as family trips often are—is based on my memories. It's a modest undertaking. Just a couple of days, only an hour or so north of the border. A test run, in fact, to see if my daughters are as excited after the fact as they have been during the planning sessions.

We'll be taking the fambulance and as is a father's prerogative I shall lull the children to sleep with my own fish stories. My Grandpa Perry's fishing trips were memorable mostly in terms of the sandwiches he made and stowed in his Little Oscar cooler alongside "fun size" Snickers candy bars. My brother John and I were grateful to Grandpa for the treat, but being under the age of ten we felt a candy bar's "fun" factor was directly proportional to its size and that the Snickers people had done some evil math. We have battled cynicism ever since.

On my mother's side, Grandpa Peterson was never much of a fisherman, but that didn't stop him from talking big. "All you need is a willow switch for a pole, some of your mother's sewing thread for a line, and a safety pin for a hook," he'd declare from his recliner in the living room as we listened with wide and believing eyes, never anticipating the disappointment ahead. "And then you just fry 'em up in a pan," he concluded, this from the man who never in his whole live-long life ever fried up anything up in a pan except maybe his tie when he leaned in to see what Grandma was cooking.

On the dark side, fishing trips can lead to everlasting family fractures. My brother John and I were still in our single-digit years when Grandpa Perry and our dad took us on a fishing trip up north. This was long before Grandpa retired and bought his Little Oscar cooler. Times were tight (although not too tight for fishin'), and so when we stopped at the bait shop John and I were thrilled to see the grown-ups returning with a cool green bottle of 7UP and a full-sized Baby Ruth candy bar. The plan was to share amongst the four of us. Little John went first. Took a bite of that candy bar and passed it to me. I took a bite and passed to Grandpa. Little John took a swig of 7UP and passed the bottle to me. I raised it halfway to my lips and stopped. What had been a bottle of crystal-clear soda was now swirling with bits of Baby Ruth.

Guess who got a whole bottle of 7UP to himself?

In the family, we refer to this as the Backwash Episode. To this day I believe he did it on purpose and it will come up at the reading of the will.

And whether we catch some on this trip or not, here is what I hope my daughters learn: Not every fish story requires a fish.

THE WAY THE STORY GOES

Well, my brother John went and ruined one of my favorite stories.

The tale as I've been telling it begins with a riff on the idea that among certain social groups (in my case, blue-collar working-class farmer/logger types) nothing is more entertaining than another person's pain, e.g., if your buddy gets hit in the head with a monkey wrench, once you've established that he's still breathing and likely able to walk again, *nothing's funnier than your buddy getting hit in the head with a monkey wrench.*

This leads me then to introduce Jerry, the quiet farmer who taught my city-bred father to farm and for whom my brothers and I often worked. Jerry was a gentle man, kind, and not given to guffawing—unless you hit your head on the silo pipe or purpled your thumbnail with a shingle hammer, at which point he dissolved into helpless giggles.

Turnabout being fair play, I have therefore enjoyed telling the story of when Jerry's best milk cow took ill. He had the vet out several times, but the cow continued to decline. Soon she could no longer stand. Then came the day Jerry realized that the cow was not going to recover, and was furthermore in physical pain. With heavy heart, he called my younger brother Jed. "Can you come over with your deer rifle," Jerry asked, "and put this poor cow out of her misery?"

Brother Jed did. Now the two men were faced with removing the corpse from the barn. Jed backed a tractor up to the door and ran a cable from the hitch, looped it around one hind leg of the cow, then slowly drew the cow from its stall as Jerry stood silently by, failing to notice that the free rear leg had become hung up on the stanchion and was being drawn back and cocked like the arm of a catapult. Jerry had one bad knee, and when the cow's hoof cleared the stanchion it whipped around and smashed Jerry right in his trick knee. As he hopped around clutching his patella, Jed stopped the tractor. "You gonna be all right?" he asked Jerry. "I think so," said Jerry, weakly.

At which point Jed said, "'Cuz I got one more shell."

Boy, that line really gets the laughs.

Then I made the mistake of telling it at a family gathering the other night. My brother John was there. He let me finish, then went right down the list: The cow wasn't sick and being treated by a vet, it had broken its front leg. It wasn't Jed who shot the cow, it was John. Jerry didn't get smacked in the knee, but rather the ankle. And it wasn't Jed or John who uttered the punch line, it was Jerry, who in fact asked, "You got one more shell?"

This was a grievous disappointment—and baffling. I can't recall hearing the story any other way than I'd told it. While I will now and then avail myself of what some call "rhetorical declamations," which in short means a storyteller (including Betty down there at the beauty shop) is allowed to rev things up for the sake of humor, the greater power comes from truth and specificity.

I suspect what happened here was the chronological equivalent of the game of telephone. I heard the story once, cogitated it for years, then began retelling it based on my own faulty recall. And gosh, I had it fine-tuned. Now what?

The fact remains, a guy got kicked by a dead cow. If I can't fashion a funny story from that, I should surrender my talking stick. And so I shall apply myself in that direction. I will polish and perfect it. I will take it to the masses.

I will never tell it within earshot of brother John.

MOM ON BOOK TOUR

As you read this, I am well into the first week of a book tour. This sounds glamorous and is indeed more than what a flat-footed clodhopper the likes of me ever had reason to hope, but in fact what we are talking about is a guy driving around Wisconsin with occasional detours into Minnesota and Illinois. Nonetheless, I travel with gratitude and the recognition that none of this would have occurred were it not for Mom.

There were the conception and birth, of course. According to the paperwork, the latter occurred in Wisconsin Rapids. As for the former, I am told by one of the parties concerned it most likely occurred during a three-day ice storm in Illinois. What this tells us is that but for a fortuitous mid-gestation relocation I came within a few brief weeks of having been born a Bears fan.

Go, Packers.

Shortly after I emerged and drew my first Dairyland air, Mom started reading to me. I liked that. A lot. So much that I bugged her to do it constantly, tugging at her elbow while she tried to read her own books. At one point she cut a deal with me, trading one chapter of *Winnie the Pooh* read aloud for a measure of time to read a chapter of her own book to herself. It was in this way she taught me to love sitting quietly with a book even before I could read one.

When I began pointing out letters, Mom sent away (Remember a time when we "sent away" for things? You do? Me too! We're old!) to a Chicago newspaper for a phonics book. We went through it page by page and when we finished I could read. (Well, *kinda*. My dad loves to tell how I pointed at the tailgate of a pickup truck and proudly recited, "F-O-R-D . . . *TRUCK!*") After that, Mom made sure we wore a regular path to the nearest small-town library in Chetek, Wisconsin. The house was forever filled with books.

Mom contributed two other critical elements to my love of reading. First, she was of a faith that forbade television—so books won out by default. Second, she was a compulsive reader, unable to sit still without looking for something to peruse, and I inherited that genetic predilection (to this day I can recite the American Dental Association spiel from the back of the tooth-paste tube, because, well, because sometimes that's the only prose within reach).

I've told these stories before, in other books and other essays, but in anticipation of this book tour have been revisiting them. This whole writing thing has been a happy accident (for me, anyway—some critics agree it was simply an accident, and fair enough, let 'er rip). I grew up a pitchforking farm kid, a football-playing knucklehead, and a decent but probably underperform-ing student. I went to college, got a nursing degree, and took work in a hospital. Rambled around the world some. Then one day I found myself paying the rent by typing.

The path to this point has been composed largely of tangents. But they all trace back to a mother who took it upon herself to share time and words with a curious child. During this book tour (for *The Scavengers*) I will be telling the story of another young child who—albeit under much more adverse circumstances than I have ever faced—loves nothing more than to sit beside her mother and share a book.

The character is fictitious. But the message between the lines is not: *Thanks, Mom.*

RESURRECTING GRANDPA'S VOICE

When my grandmother died, she left behind a mystery. As do many family mysteries, it resided in a cardboard box tucked in the corner of a closet, only to be discovered during death's disbursements. It is a brown paperboard mailer, hand-addressed to my grandmother. The street number is appended with "½" so I deduce she was living in an apartment with my toddler father when the mailman dropped it through the slot.

A small square has been cut from the upper right-hand corner of the mailer. The size and location of the excision, as well as the residual amputated tail of the cancellation mark, suggests someone—perhaps Grandma, for her collection—removed the stamp. A banner running the bottom border of the mailer bears the words "DO NOT FOLD." The return address is left blank, but above the space provided it is announced that the contents within arrive "THROUGH COURTESY OF PEPSI-COLA."

And then, in script, running at an angle along the left-hand border: *"This is a recorded message from your Man in Service."*

The first time I read those words, my heart leapt. Grandpa served in World War II. A Navy man. Went ashore in Iwo Jima (having served as a yeoman, he liked to joke that he stormed the beach "armed with a typewriter," although in time we grandchildren learned that the story was of course nowhere near so benign). Based on the script and the shape of the packet I assumed it must contain a phonograph disc, and the idea that we might be able to hear him speak to us directly from the past was tantalizing. What would he say? Would he speak of the war?

Would we hear fear in his voice? Would he leave instructions for how to fix the latch on the screen door?

But there was another reason I was eager to hear this recording: Grandpa survived the war but shortly afterward developed cancer of the larynx. Surgeons removed a portion of his vocal cords, leaving a rasp in his voice. I remember Grandma saying Grandpa loved to sing in the choir, and the loss of song saddened him. Sometime later the cancer recurred, and doctors removed more of his vocal cords. I still remember vividly the day we grandkids gathered around to hear him speak after that surgery. His voice was a hoarse whisper, and would so remain until his death.

And now, here in my hands, was our chance to hear Grandpa speak in the voice we grandchildren had never heard.

I drew out the disk, and my heart sank. It was cracked and crazed, the entire playing surface riven with zigzag fissures. I held it at the edges and studied it a bit, then returned it to the sleeve. There was simply no way it would play. I'd have to be content with it as a simple tchotchke. Just something to look at now and then. I locked it away in a small fire safe and forgot about it.

Then one day a longtime acquaintance mentioned that he had started an audio preservation company. I mentioned the Pepsi-Cola recording, and he said he was willing to see what sound he might be able to resurrect from the record (he said it was a "cellulose-nitrate lacquer recordable disc," and that they were known to deteriorate). I reiterated how badly damaged it was, but he persisted, so I packaged the record in roughly six square feet of bubble-wrap, waterproofing, and a crush-proof box and sent it on its way.

◆ ◆ ◆

This is my father's first memory of his father: The little boy is waiting with his mother for a train due to arrive in downtown Eau Claire, Wisconsin. World War II is nearly over, and the boy's father—all my life I knew him as Grandpa—has returned stateside after serving in Iwo Jima. Bound from San Francisco to New

York, where he will be stationed until his discharge, the young Navy veteran has been granted a brief leave.

He is bound for home.

The little boy waiting carries no memories of his father. The separation of war has deprived him of this. And yet, he has seen photos. Always the adults were showing him photos, including those of a young man in uniform. This is your dad, they would say. And so, when the train comes to a stop and the passengers debark, the little boy fixes his eyes on the trim sailor descending the stairs and knows: that is my dad.

The little boy is in his eighth decade now, and he carries that scene clearly to this day.

I carry a scene of my own: Grandpa, sitting at our kitchen table, his voice breathy and hoarse, the adults having some discussion concerning surgery or hospitals. My little brother, saggy-diapered, moving cautiously closer, listening intently, and finally saying, "Grandpa . . . why are you whispering?" And then the adults—Grandpa included—laughing, and me, as a child, feeling relief. Something had gone wrong, but the laughter meant it would be okay. At least that's how I remember it.

When our ancestors pass, we are left to carry their history, and we do so with our stories. Even if we have no reason to embellish or fabricate, no desire to relay anything but the solid facts, we quickly discover bubbles in the amber that distort our perspective. When I found the phonograph recording among Grandma's things, it triggered a discussion of family history, and it was interesting to see how our memories did—and did not—match up. I assumed the message was recorded before Grandpa left for Iwo Jima; my father and his sister thought it must have been made after he returned. Some remembered Grandpa having only one throat surgery; others remembered two, but on dates a decade apart. Perhaps this is why an object like the Pepsi-Cola recording is so dear: Whatever we might remember, however we might remember it, here is the person, available to speak directly from the past—and, in this case, in a voice most of the family has never heard.

The disc was a cracked and fragile mess, but through a combined miracle of vintage equipment and digital technology, my audio preservationist friend was able to liberate the message trapped within the fractured grooves. When he called with the good news, I asked that he not reveal what he had heard, so that my first listen might be without expectation—although I did ask if he heard anything that might rock the family boat. He assured me he did not, and shortly I was in possession of a CD carrying Grandpa's voice in digital form.

I loaded it into the player and pushed play.

The recording begins with a thin electronic squeal followed by a muffled *tha-thump, tha-thump, tha-thump* repeating itself at seventy-eight revolutions per minute. Even this sound is remarkable, given the tenuous condition of the original disc. The audio preservationist has performed a miracle.

Grandpa has been gone for over twenty years. To this day, when we quote him in favorite family stories we adopt his sandpapery whisper. The idea that I am about to hear his original voice for the first time is tantalizing.

At first the voice is unintelligible. I make out the words, *". . . in San Francisco, California. All right, Dal . . . "* Grandpa's name was Dallas, but he went by Dal. So this first voice belongs to the person running the recording booth.

But then: *"Hello Wanda, how are ya?"* That's him! Wanda was my grandmother! The voice sounds slightly speeded up and stilted. Like the old black-and-white newsreels.

"How are you Billy, you bum!" You can hear the smile in his voice as he speaks to my father—a toddler who knows his father's face only from photographs. *"I'm talkin' to ya from Calif—from, ah, San Francisco, California. First leave I had since I've been out here, eight hour leave, gonna go back in the morning."*

Now, in the way he pronounces "California," and "morning," I can hear the northern Wisconsin inflections and more familial tones—those of my father and brothers.

"I asked the, ah, lieutenant for a week or two off, but he wouldn't

let me do that, so I thought the best thing I could do is send you my voice. We got the war about won out here, as soon as it's over I'll be home."

Now each sentence is broken by a pause. I can't tell if this is due to emotion or the alien experience of sitting in a booth knowing he had a limited amount of time to speak to a family from whom he'd been so long absent.

"You gotta keep the home fires burning."

Another pause, nearly five seconds long. In some of these setups, tongue-tied servicemen were provided a selection of scripted lines. I'm not sure if Grandpa was perusing one of these or simply unsure of what to say.

"Keep yer chin up, keep in there pitchin'."

That one makes sense. He was a big baseball fan, and I remember him using the pitching phrase.

"Won't be long."

He sounds like he only half believes this.

"Like to have ya out here with me, I don't know if that'll be permissible or not, but . . ."

Now the longest pause yet, followed by a soft, wry *"Ha!"* and then something unintelligible.

"So long now, and I'll see ya . . . soon."

"Bye, Billy, you bum."

Then it is just *tha-thump, tha-thump,* and then, silence.

Thanks to this digital age, the message makes the family rounds in a matter of hours, triggering a flurry of emailed remembrances. As messages go, it's hardly dramatic. But now my elder daughter is at our kitchen table, a smartphone in her hand. She once composed a school history project about Grandpa, who died long before she was born. She included a photo of him in his Iwo Jima foxhole, quoted a telegram he sent from the front, and wrote a report. Now she taps the smartphone screen, and somewhere back in time her great-grandfather steps into a booth, and, propelling himself into the future, says the most magical thing: *"I thought the best thing I could do is send you my voice . . ."*

REVISITING TOM

"Lemme show ya my latest project!"

Last thing I did before leaving on book tour recently was visit my neighbor Tom. One of the characters in my new novel—a fictitious but alacritous octogenarian named Toad—was drawn directly from my observations of Tom, so I had come to share a copy of the book. But it had also been a while since I'd dropped in to pay my respects. Tom is into his second year of life without his wife, Arlene. They were married for sixty years. Every day he feels the echo of her absence. You wouldn't, I don't think, want to bring up the term "closure" with Tom any time soon.

So it was good, after I handed him the book, to hear him utter that familiar invitation. "Lemme show ya my latest project!" is one of Tom's most reliable utterances, and it is reliably worthy of follow-up. This, after all, is a man who builds his own fully operational cannons from scratch. In the winter, he clears his driveway using a tractor-mounted snowblower he cobbled together from bisected well casings, parts from an old hammer mill, and the bull wheel from a vintage grain binder. The last time he invited me to view his latest project it was a multigeared roller grinder contraption intended to grind his cannon powder to a finer texture, thus increasing its explosive power.

Today, however, the latest project is a cuckoo clock, dissembled into countless parts and spread across the dining room table. The cuckoo clock was a favorite possession of Tom and Arlene. It hung on the wall for decades, the mechanism ticking, the pendulum squeaking, and every hour the cuckoo springing forth to mark another hour passed in their lives together. Arlene loved to point the clock out to visitors, and Tom would always tell the story of the time the minute hand spun loose and he and Arlene had to drive over to Mondovi to get the parts to fix it. Tom had been a little off during that drive to Mondovi. He kept crossing the centerline with the Crown Vic, and a policeman had stopped him for it. A day later he wasn't able to keep his balance and fell over while fetching the mail. When it happened again the next day, Arlene made him go to the hospital, where the doctors discovered a bleed on his brain. For a while it looked like Arlene would be the one living alone, but Tom made a full recovery, both he and the cuckoo clock ticking along.

But now something is wrong with the clock again. "It'll *kook*, but it won't *koo!*" says Tom. "See, how it works, is it has two miniature bellows." He points into the housing. "That one there, that makes the *kook* sound. But this one here, the bellows are shot." He holds up what looks to be a small wooden flapper attached to a rectangular chamber. I can see traces of deteriorated paper.

"I tried replacing the bellows, but the paper I had was too thick," says Tom. "So I got my micrometer, and I measured the thickness of the original paper. It's seven-thousandths." He then reveals that he has spent the better part of the afternoon driving around town in his Crown Victoria, popping into convenience store restrooms and restaurant bathrooms to collect samples of their paper towels. "See now," he says, showing me a sample with a number written on it, "McDonald's, they're runnin' a four-thousandths sheet. That's too thin."

I am hardly hearing him now, so slack-jawed am I at the idea of him running in and out of all those restrooms to collect all that paper toweling.

I've told this story quite a bit on tour. Folks get a nice laugh out of it. I'll tell Tom about it when I get back. I'll owe him another visit by then. And if I know the man, if I arrive at the top of the hour, I'll hear a *kook* and a *koo*.

OLD WAY OUT OF TOWN

There was a moment before the funeral when I reached for the suit that hangs with the tie in my closet. Then I drew my hand back and figured jeans and flannel would do. It was good then, when I arrived at St. Jude's, to see so many others similarly attired, and the soloist wearing overalls.

St. Jude's is my hometown Catholic church. The church was "suppressed" by the bishop thirteen years ago, which is to say the consecrated bread was removed and the parish disbanded, but the building can still be used for some services, funerals included. As it is the most spacious worship structure in town, the Catholics have long made it available to other denominations when overflow is a concern, as was the case for the funeral I attended.

The casket was homemade. Pine and walnut, with antler handles. The body in repose was that of an old-timer we all called Ike. If you're local you know that's not the name his mama gave him but it's the one that stuck for eighty-eight years. On this his final appearance he too was clad in overalls. His head rested on a camouflage-print pillow, and his hands were encased in the same loose work gloves he always wore in the days when he was farming and carpentering. As I remember it, he would crack a joke, then waggle his hands in those gloves while everyone laughed.

It was good to sit in a church named after the patron saint of lost causes. In a society that glorifies winners, I gratefully carry a candle for St. Jude. There is comfort in the idea of someone dedicated to reaching out to those of us who proceed at a perpetual stumble. I am not a religious fellow, but I hope I am a reflective fellow, and if you find yourself in a church pew in honor of a neighbor who knew you when you were just a kid with a cowlick, well, you might ought to ponder your progress. I know when I looked around that church and saw the overflowing multitude who came to honor the man in the casket, I adjusted my measuring stick.

I'm over fifty now, so if I wrote an essay every time I attended or got news of a funeral, I'd be well on my way to a fat anthology. I can't, of course. And in this small space I can't do justice to Ike and his life (nor his faithful surviving wife, Ramona, without whom . . .). I'm not the same little boy I was when Ike was the neighbor who entertained us by making his tractor backfire when he roared past our farm. I've strayed in geographic and other fashions. I am my own lost cause. But in that church, surrounded by people who populated my most formative years, in a crowd where jeans are just fine, where a man can be buried in his gloves and overalls, I was, as ever, grateful to be of and from a place like this. After they latched that homemade casket, we gathered in the annex for food and talk, and then I walked across the icy street to my car. On a whim, I took the old road out of town, the one we all drove back before they punched the four-lane through.

GODFATHER

Last Sunday I became a godfather. Again. The first time around I was still in my teens. Right out of the gate my goddaughter Amy Lynn faced life-threatening cardiac surgeries, and I recall her father and I at her bedside only months removed from Friday night football games, realizing life can run up the score on short notice indeed.

When she was a toddler, Amy Lynn gave me a crayon drawing of an apple tree, executed in the standard style: brown trunk, green leaves, red apples, spiky yellow sun in a blue sky. It contained one visual anomaly: a tiny, very carefully inscribed square, done in pencil. I was in nursing school and had just completed a 300-level child psychology course, so I immediately homed in on the anomalous square as a subliminal message of perhaps dire import. At the first opportunity I sat down with Amy Lynn and asked her to tell me about the drawing, and she did—in the sunniest of terms. Then, when the time was right, I pointed to the square, and as gently as I could, asked, "And what is this?"

She looked at me quizzically for a moment, and then, as if addressing the dimmest of all godfathers, said, "It's a *square.*"

It is one of the resonant regrets of my life that I allowed time and distance and life in general to separate Amy Lynn and me. We reunited on her wedding day, and have seen each other a handful of times since, but I fear I have lapsed again. I find some consolation in reporting that for decades the apple tree picture hung framed above my writing desk, but the last time I moved, it wound up in a box that has yet to be unpacked.

All of this was on my mind as I stood in the church vowing to remain present in the life of my newborn nephew and watch over him should harm befall his parents. His mother is from Fall Creek, Wisconsin, and his father is from Chitré, Panama. Mi cuñado, I call the father: my brother-in-law. After the ceremony mi cuñado told me that once I became his son's padrino he and I became compadres. I knew compadre meant buddy or pal, but when I looked it up in the translator later, I discovered there is a deeper definition, essentially meaning that swaddled infant has joined we two men for life.

On the drive home, I kept thinking of Amy Lynn. When I arrived, I wrote a letter to the priest who baptized my nephew and requested he send me a copy of the baptismal vows. Again, I was thinking of Amy Lynn, and that I need to keep those vows in sight so I don't lose track of my responsibilities in any sense. I also thought I should go down to the pole barn and dig around in my stash of boxes until I found Amy Lynn's framed drawing. And then I thought I should get beyond self-serving symbolism and contact Amy Lynn. And so even as I write this, I have learned that some of the health troubles she faced all those decades ago have resurfaced in the direst sense. I don't know what help a wayward godfather can be. But I will not wait for news.

And the next time mi cuñado—mi compadre—hands me his son, I will cradle the boy in my arms, look into his brown eyes and think, little ahijado, I have vowed to watch over you, but already you are watching over me.

GETTING LACED

We all wish to begin the day in victory, so I was quite pleased when I rose this morning and discovered I could still tie my shoes.

I don't intend the joke quite as broadly as it might seem; one takes nothing for granted in this life, including the ability to complete what my nursing school instructors used to refer to as "ADLs," which was an abbreviation for "activities of daily living." If, at daybreak, I remain able to tie my shoes, I count it as the first of many moments in the day to come when thanks are owed.

I learned to tie my shoes thanks to a man named Uncle Chris. Technically he was my great-uncle once removed, or something of the sort, but everyone in the family simply called him Uncle Chris. Uncle Chris was a bespectacled, skinny man of great physical and intellectual energy. He had a way in conversation—and I remember feeling this even as a tot at the annual Fourth of July family reunion—of making you feel as if you were providing the interesting half of the conversation, even as he proved otherwise. A self-taught engineer who lived in the Chicago suburbs and designed industrial ovens, he and his family dwelled in a house he built himself using only three-foot lengths of wood salvaged from wooden ammunition crates. There were also stories of him competing in one-hundred-mile bicycle races in the 1940s. He built his own camping trailer, and every summer, he and Aunt Rae rented a lake cabin in Wisconsin, and as a young boy I would be allowed to spend a day or two at the campground with Uncle Chris and his family. I have vivid memories of sailing the lake on a twin-hull catamaran, designed and built—naturally—by Uncle Chris in his suburban backyard.

On a Sunday morning during one of the lake weekends, I got dressed for church and asked Uncle Chris to tie my shoes. "Oh, it's time you learned to do that for yourself!" he said, and rather than feeling chastised, I felt like he was inviting me on a grand adventure. So Aunt Rae drove, and Uncle Chris and I sat in the back. I can still see my little wingtip propped on the drive-shaft hump as Uncle Chris patiently coached me through the knots and bows, then undid the laces so I could start again. I'm not sure if I had it licked by the time we got to church, but I know by the time I got back home I had it down pat and was excited to show Mom. That fall Uncle Chris and Aunt Rae went back to Illinois and I went off to kindergarten. I still have my Initial Progress Report, and under the section "Handles Wraps & Ties Shoes," Mrs. Amodt put a check mark beside "Independently."

How many times, I wonder, have I tied my shoes since then? Before church, before grade school Christmas concerts, junior high football games, before my first date, on the first day of college, in other countries, before funerals and birthdays, on the day of my marriage (okay, that day I wore steel-toed boots, not shoes, but I still had to tie them), and—perhaps most significantly—on nearly every given morning of nearly every regular old day.

It's on those regular old days that I am most likely to think of Uncle Chris and the legacy inherent in the things we do by habit. This morning when I rose and pulled on my boots, snugged up the laces, and then, turning the process over to that autopilot known as muscle memory—*flick, tug, flick, flick, loop, tug, switch feet, repeat*—tied two bows, and then stomped off into whatever was to follow, giving thanks for the most basic of things, and for Uncle Chris—kind, goofy, and brilliant right up until cancer took him twenty years ago—who taught me how to lace up and face the day on solid footing.

FIRE CALL

I was two sentences into this column when the fire pager went off. I had just done the morning chicken chores and was going to compose a piece deciphering the animal tracks I saw in the fresh half-inch of snow, but now, as I scribbled down the address and pulled on my boots, I was thinking of other things.

I have been privileged to serve in some modest capacity with fire and emergency medical services since shortly after I graduated from nursing school in the late 1980s, whereupon I quickly discovered that whenever there was an injury or medical issue, someone would turn to me and say, "Hey—you're a nurse . . . ," on the assumption that I had training in these specifics, when in fact—while my nursing school was terrific—ours was a general preparation. One day, upon hearing an ambulance siren during my hospital shift, I thought, *Well, I should take an EMT class, so I know what to do when there's trouble.* I got my brother to enroll with me. When my mother heard, she said, "I've always wanted to do something with my boys," and she enrolled also. I shall never forget the time during our extrication training when I looked across the college shop floor and saw her armed with the Jaws of Life, ripping the front door off a Gremlin. My father always treated her with respect; perhaps now I was learning why.

Still living in my college town, I started working weekends for a private ambulance service. Picked up a lot of experience. Saw death and destruction close up. On those early calls, my hands really shook. But I soon learned that once I got into action, the shaking stopped. I was relieved, because in the world of rescue, knowledge and action are essential but rendered useless if you can't keep your cool.

When I moved back to my hometown in 1995, it seemed only natural to join the ambulance service. I also took my firefighter training so that I could serve on that branch. For a stretch there, my mother, two of my brothers, and my sister-in-law were all members of the department. Sometimes it was hard to distinguish a barn fire from a family reunion.

In 2007 I moved from my hometown to a farm in the adjacent county. First thing I did was join up with the local fire and rescue service, where I still serve as an emergency medical responder. I'm on the road a lot, so I don't make a pile of calls like I did in the old days, but when I'm home the pager is on, and when it beeps and the call goes out, it's a privilege to respond.

I invoke the term "privilege" with intention. People ask me sometimes: "You still doing that EMT stuff?" as if maybe it was a stage I was going through, when in fact, apart from breathing and a few other basics, I can't think of any other pursuit I've stuck with as long—over twenty-five years now. It's a relationship sustained by more than flashing lights and adrenaline. You do it for the action and excitement, sure, but you also do it because somewhere along the line you learn the emergency services reinforce your own mortality—and rather than being a downer, this actually enriches your appreciation for what life allows. You also do it because you feel a bond with those along with whom you serve—today when I pulled up on that fire scene it made me proud to see familiar faces doing good works. And above all, you wear that pager because you know one day it will be you or yours in need of help, and you hope you've stored up some karma for whoever answers that call.

We were on the fire ground for a long time. I can't say much about it except that everyone got out alive, and that's goal number 1. Then there was a medical call on the way home. By the time I returned to my desk it was late in the afternoon and the workday was pretty much shot. I gave up on writing that column about tracks in the snow, but not before plugging the pager into the charger, so when trouble calls it will let me know, and it will be my privilege to go.

APPLE GOLF

Well, Great-Grandma's 7-iron is busted for good.

Great-Grandma (my grandma, but as this story includes the youngest generation of the matrilineal line, we will shift the honorific) has been gone for a decade now, and probably played her last game of golf a decade or two prior to that. I'm not sure how I ended up with her 7-iron, but I did, and I'm glad, because Grandma was a tiny lady, so the club is short and a good fit for my eight-year-old daughter.

We are not a golfing family in the classical sense. I haven't teed off for eighteen holes since the first Clinton administration, and even then it was a shank-errific one-off tour of adjacent foliage. A member of the family who lived on our farm previously, however, was an avid golfer—so avid, in fact, that he used our ridge for a driving range. I kick up striped golf balls in the valley below while hunting, and discover them perched like dimpled hailstones atop the dirt whenever I till the oat patch. In addition to all the scavenger hunt golf balls, this golfer left behind a clutch of old clubs down in the pole barn, one of which I was using last night when I joined my daughter in the yard for a vigorous round of clodhopper apple golf.

The primary purpose of clodhopper apple golf is to clear the yard of wormy, bespotted, and otherwise compromised windfalls. There are no rules, other than try to smack the apples in the general direction of the chicken run so they can peck at the pieces. My daughters and I have previously accomplished this by teeing up apples on a stick and smacking them into the pig pasture with a softball bat. Fun and all, but we no longer have pigs, and golfing the apples eliminates any need to bend over and pick anything up. Just walk and whack. Both methods are cheaper than going to the movies. The world is rich with diverse entertainments.

For the purpose, I favor a medium iron that provides a touch of lift while still delivering decent length and sufficient saucing. "Saucing" is a technical term used to express the ratio of chunks to juice produced when the club face contacts the fruit. A nice long drive is a delight to observe, but for purposes of spectacle and feeding the maximum amount of chickens per swing you want a balance of spritz and bits. The term is also verbified in moments of excitement, as in, "Dad! I really *sauced* it!"

Armed with Great-Grandma's stubby club, the child had a fine time whacking away. At first she made apple contact about 10 percent of the time (there was a lot of scubbing and excavating, but ours is a sod patch of a yard in which replacing your divot has no noticeable effect, so who cares—plus, *laughter*) but gradually her accuracy improved and the chickens were zipping hither and yon in pursuit of apple shrapnel. So happy was she that when the club snapped—turns out the shaft had rusted from within—she looked at me with wide eyes and then, rather than dismay, she dissolved into laughter. We took a picture of the busted club beside an exploded apple, then it was time for teeth brushing, books, and bed. In the morning she'd be off to her first day of school. Later when I went out to close up the coop, day was settling into night, summer was settling into fall, and the air was apple sweet.

SHOOTING THE BREEZE

One of the things you discover when living at the terminus of a dead-end country road is that a certain segment of the population is possessed of an odd dyslexic-type disorder in which they interpret a yellow diamond DEAD END sign as a DUMP HERE sign. Several times a year we are greeted by all manner of trash and unwanteds tipped out by the mailbox or slung into the wooded verge.

My neighbor Denny lives right at the base of the hill where our dead-end road commences, and since he retired he has made it his part-time hobby to keep an eye out for these landfill flouts. A while back he saw an unfamiliar van head up our hill and decided to investigate. He zipped up there on his four-wheeler and caught a pair of knuckleheads making their escape after chucking a bunch of electronics into the ditch. Denny blocked the road and made them load it all back up while he sat there watching them, astride his four-wheeler like some Old West sheriff.

Given this history, when I motored out our tree-lined drive last night only to encounter an upended recliner and sofa sectional on the shoulder it wasn't a complete surprise. In fact, our sofa is pretty much shot, so I slowed down for a quick look on the off chance it might match our nonexistent drapes. Unfortunately whoever did the dumping apparently did so at speed, and while the cushions looked good, the understructure had not survived.

Leaving this windfall behind, I drove to the bottom of the hill and hung a right. Spotting Denny in his yard, I pulled into his driveway and lowered my passenger side window. "Hey!" I yelled. Denny looked up from what he was doing. "You missin' yer couch?"

Denny came over and leaned through the window. I told him about the fractured furniture. He shook his head. "What kinda person thinks that's okay?" I said, and Denny shook his head again, and said he'd found a refrigerator and a toilet in the ditch recently. But then in defense of the common man Denny started reciting how much they charge you when you take a load of junk to the dump these days, and what a rigamarole it is to dispose of appliances, and in fact there are plenty of folks who just don't have that in their budget, let alone their wallet.

That led us to discuss burn barrel fees and how they led to a proliferation of "fire pits" and then we veered off into how it came to be that his ditch out in front of the house there was all ash-blackened and it turns out that story is a real knee-slapper that Denny admits began when he uttered the words "I wonder if this stuff'll burn?" (the pyromaniac equivalent of "Here, hold my beer!") and shortly led to him running a one-man bucket brigade back and forth between the ditch and his wife's koi pond, and how when she asked him what he was doing he basically said *no time to talk!*

Then we got on to what mighta killed his three roosters and pretty soon we'd shot a good twenty to thirty minutes through the car window and when I finally pulled out of the driveway headed for where I was headed in the first place I thought, *Well, I wish people wouldn't be grotesque litterbugs, and whoever dumped that living room set I wish I'd a caught 'em when I had my snowplow and some stubble on, I coulda maybe put a little fear in 'em,* but then again they wound up giving me a reason to stop in and shoot the breeze with Denny, and I'll remember that ditch fire story a lot longer than I'll remember that sofa.

SLEDDING PARTY

It was a good day for sledding. The snow was deep and temperatures were mild. Uncle Mike shut the beefers in the barn so we
could leave the gates open on our way through the pasture to
the hill. We moved along in a bundled herd, the young ones chat-
tering and scampering, the grownups following in a lower gear.

We gather for the family sledding party once a year. Have been
for I don't know how long—the years outpace recollection. Uncle
Mike and Aunt Sal have the perfect hill: big enough to achieve to-
bogganing speed and a few stocking-cap-over-snowboots tumbles
but not terminal-velocity vertiginous and emptying at the base
into a flat deceleration and collection zone.

I am old enough to remember when sledding was mostly limited to runner sleds and steel saucers. In fact, some of my fondest
winter memories are of my brothers and sisters and I skidding off
the lean-to roof in our dented old saucer, a conveyance as beat
up as a used gladiator's shield (as it was sometimes deployed
during lath sword fights in the warmer seasons). We had to duck
halfway down the roof so as not to clothesline ourselves on the
decrepit but very much alive electrical wire that sagged across
the luge path, then brace as we went airborne and dropped to
the snowbank below. Reliving this memory on the sledding hill
yesterday, my youngest brother Jed (now a forty-something father of five) said that as he was always relegated to going last, by
the time his turn came around the landing pad had been tamped

solid and his predominant memory—vivid, if not cherished—is of the vertebral shock upon impact.

These days we don't spring back like we used to—there are trick backs and weak legs and inflexible hamstrings among us—but we still join our children on the slope, hooting and hollering and exulting in the most spectacular tumbles. In what is perhaps a lesson on the limited value of sentimentality in the real world, our kids spend most of their time sledding not on sleds, but on slick plastic contraptions infused with unnaturally fluorescent colors and seizure-inducing graphics apparently designed with the specific intent of irritating anyone over forty. And yet even the cheapest of these provides a thrill tough to match on the old Rosebud, no matter how well you scrub the runners with an old candle.

We still run a couple of old wooden toboggans. I recognize one of them as the same the grumpy teenaged version of me used to haul hay bales to the sheep when they were snowbound in the back forty (I grumped, but deep inside I felt myself a heroic frontiersman). The toboggans make for the best team runs, bunches of us nested front to back and hooting at every swoop and dip until we glide to a stop or tip off sideways, everybody disentangling and laughing through the sting-burn of snow on our cheeks.

Uncle Mark brought his snowmobile and made big loops from the bottom of the hill back to the top, dragging sleds and sledders back up for run after run until finally the specific gravity of Aunt Sal's pork and beans barbecue simmering on the stove began to exert its pull, and one by one each child made a final descent and struck out for the house. From atop the hill my brother John and I watched from a distance as my younger daughter and her cohort cousin walked side-by-side across the white gulf below, two little snowsuited compadres in full happy jabber. We smiled to think the two tots were already outfitted with memories, something against which to measure the future, whatever it might bring. Over the years there has been some untimely mortality in our family, and it was impossible not to think of the ones we've lost. But when Uncle Mike went out to close the gates and release the beefers, the empty hill above him was crisscrossed with tracks, a hieroglyphic open to the sky, reading *Whatever comes, we had this day.*

APPRECIATION

THE BLIND BOYS

My daughter and I crossed the border and were in Minnesota now, jammed into the Cedar Cultural Center with the rest of the full house come to see the Blind Boys of Alabama. The history of the group stretches back to the 1930s and is personified by Jimmy Carter, somewhere in the high eighties and the only founding member still actively touring. Mr. Carter frankly hollered the roof off the place, stomping and roaring and in the company of his colleagues raising a joyful noise indeed.

Our trip was the closing of a circle opened nearly a year ago when the Blind Boys of Alabama waded through the snow to record a new album in—of all places—rural Fall Creek, Wisconsin. By chance I had a small involvement in the project and as a result my daughter and I were able to observe a portion of the recording session. When I heard the tour in support of the album would be passing through Minneapolis, I thought it would be nice to hear the studio music live.

The room was packed, and after making their way to the stage in the fashion that has become their custom—in a line, each man resting a hand on the shoulder of the man ahead—the men sang from their chairs and sometimes leapt to their feet. When one of the singers drew too near the edge of the stage, the guitar player would guide him backward while the bass and drums held the beat and the organist filled. There was joy and power in the room and the people were often out of their seats. Our vantage point was from along a back wall, and I was struck as always by the mystery of live performance. How despite all the history of the group and thousands of shows in all settings and countries and circumstance—the only thing that matters is the show happening *now* and how it resonates with each person present in their own way and time.

I make a lot of humorous hay about being in over my head as a parent, but of course it's true and of course it is not always fodder for chuckles. You do what you can: the basics, the things you learned from your parents, the things that seem to work for other parents. And then sometimes you simply provide experiences and hope they'll have some subterranean positive effect.

My daughter was twelve when we saw the Blind Boys in studio. She is a teenager now and developing her own tastes and preferences. I don't wish to lumber her with the implication that she best henceforth immerse herself in nonagenarian gospel blues. But I am grateful for this music, because over the course of the past year it has led us to conversations that touched on faith and race and age and the nature of harmony, and—when the Blind Boys hit a fever pitch or a certain pleading note—turn to each other in shared wide-eyed wonder. She will go back to her iTunes and digital dub step and streaming insta-hits and any other number of cultural doodads that will explode and dissipate in a matter of days or in lingering increments of last-dollar reunion tours or—let's be generationally fair here—becoming a lasting part of a new cultural lexicon. But perhaps somewhere in the mix she will carry a memory of the night her old dad took her to see the even older singers and she found herself in a room with humans enjoying the company of other humans. Perhaps she will carry within her some sense of context, some formative tincture that will color her perception well beyond music.

And perhaps—should the day ever come when she needs it—she will recall that sometimes joy is to be found outside our standard deviation.

WORKING WITH MUSICIANS

Some time ago a neighbor who does some songwriting asked if I might help out with a project. I said yes, thanks, and did. Mostly my job was to listen and type. This led to my spending a lot of time in the company of musicians, observing them in the manner of an untrained anthropologist. Many of them were very hip and cutting-edge and subversively stylish and whatnot, and a few of them have names that elicit *oohs* and *aahs* all around the world and some have won Grammys and some might win them soon and others of them you will have heard in television advertisements for Volkswagens. They were by and large an equanimous bunch, if a little drifty, impulsive, and easily distracted by the latest distortion pedal or free food. A lot of their music I don't get, which did nothing to impede my enjoyment in watching them at their work. Craft is craft, whether in the shaping of a song or the fitting of bathroom tile. The older I get the more deeply I believe "getting" things is far less important than experiencing them with a spirit of appreciation. In fact, the fear of not "getting" things may be a leading impediment to happiness and certainly leads to chronic stiffening of the spine.

In my thirties I went through an extended stage in which I felt compelled to warn folks away from the vacuity of then-contemporary country music. In particular I was agitating for "alternative country," which in my opinion served my modern and artistic sensibilities while properly doffing its non–cowboy hat to classic country stalwarts, or, as I call them, "the one-namers":

Waylon and Willie. Buck and Merle. George and Tammy. Loretta. Dolly. Of course this was nothing more than my oft-remarked creeping codgerism kicking in early, although—I cannot lie—I take guilty delight in having written the following line: "Johnny Paycheck is to Kenny Chesney as corn whiskey is to wine coolers."

As you can see over a decade and innumerable beach-bro hits later, Mr. Chesney's career did not waver in the face of my wit. Should we ever meet I will apologize personally. Then we'll rap out a nice set of ab crunches. If he wishes, I'll hold his ankles.

In time one learns to reserve the high horse for only very special occasions involving apple picking, and even then it's likely best left in the stable. As father to a teenaged daughter I am now familiar with a wide range of music targeted for ears less droopy than mine, and I can't always say I like what I hear, but beyond discussion of pertinent lyrical content, I keep the preaching to a minimum. Taste has a way of sorting itself out over time. "Dad!" said the teenager excitedly, "have you ever heard of Garth Brooks? His music is so much better than that stuff on the radio today! He does *real* country!"

That is not exactly how I wrote it up in 1996. But I'll let her discover that on her own. She is conversant in Lightnin' Hopkins, so one takes solace. Somewhere in the past I also wrote that it is silly to say bad things about pop music. Among the many things that shape our taste is time itself. And whatever proud stance I took back in the day, I also accidentally learned all the words to those Garth Brooks songs, which means my daughter and I can sing together in the pickup truck today.

Also: the local "classic country" station is now playing early Kenny Chesney. Which is to say, in the course of history, Kenny and entropy win.

See you at the beach.

REMEMBERING BEN LOGAN

I received the news of author Ben Logan's death while I was in a hotel room many miles from my home. Naturally I flashed back to his book *The Land Remembers,* but more specifically I flashed back to a childhood memory of reading Mr. Logan's book as I reclined on an old bedstead wedged into a corner of our farmhouse porch. I recalled midday summer sun filtering through needled white pine crowns, warm breeze filtering through the screen door, and the *chip-chip* of sparrows echoing from the barnyard.

It is an overdue blessing of our age that simplistic cultural summaries no longer pass as sufficient, and so on those occasions when I am asked to address the Wisconsin experience (usually when outside the state), I try to point out that despite persistent images it's not all red barns, green fields, and black-and-white cows. The inner-city Milwaukee experience, the suburban La Crosse experience, the Great Lakes shoreline experience—these are no less the Wisconsin experience than Alice in Dairyland scarfing cheese curds at a Friday night fish fry before the polka dance (I offer this with apologies to the real Alice in Dairyland, whom I have met and on my honor she was doing none of the things just described).

That said, if—as I was—you were raised in a world of red barns, green fields, and black-and-white cows, then you know Ben Logan got it right. He evoked a people, a place, and a time with perfect pitch. No straining, no false drama, just clear, beautiful scene upon scene. (As a guy known to use three pages to describe a shovel, I sometimes think of Ben Logan and a little voice inside my head says, *Maybe just say it's a shovel.*)

Perhaps the greater testament to Logan's writing was his ability to convey those things with which we were not familiar. I am thinking in this instance of topography: Logan's was a landscape of valleys and ridges; mine was swamps and flatland. And yet, Logan wrote the land in such a way that I felt the Driftless Area long before I ever saw it—and when I did finally travel to the southwestern corner of the state, it seemed a reunion. I suspect there are thousands of readers out there who feel the same no matter from where they hail.

I did a lot of reading on that old porch of ours. My dad, who did not treat us like free labor but did expect us to pitch in, once said he lost more man hours to my books addiction than to "football, pickup trucks, and girls combined." Even now as I recall myself lazing through *The Land Remembers,* I have this image of my father hard at work and wondering when I was going to get around to cleaning the calf pens. And yet—I suspect due to some benevolent intervention by my mother—he allowed me time off from our farm to read about another farm. I had not the slightest inkling that I would one day turn to Ben Logan's work as a source of guidance in creating my own, but there I was, quite unwittingly preparing for the future with a book of memories.

I met Ben Logan once. I thanked him as a reader, and I thanked him as a writer. I tried to keep it simple and short. You know: call a shovel a shovel, and move on. He was gracious, but even so I was left with the nagging feeling that I had failed to convey the depth of my appreciation. How do you *prove* to someone how their work has affected you without descending into fan-babble?

Perhaps it is this: In my little office over the garage, there is a set of bookshelves. On one of the shelves is a well-worn copy of *The Land Remembers.* I know its location by heart. I have read it many times.

And I am not done reading it.

TASTING POETRY

Yesterday I found myself in the position of requesting permission from a poet. Specifically, I was asking to weave two lovely lines of "On Listening to the Two-Headed Lady Blow Her Horn" by Honorée Fanonne Jeffers (from *The Gospel of Barbecue*) into my next novel. You could say my request was based on surrender; in eleven words Jeffers was able to convey something I—given hundreds of pages to work with—could not.

Most of my childhood poetic knowledge was drawn from Dr. Seuss, a 1936 edition of *The Best Loved Poems of the American People* (I favored the "Humor and Whimsey" section), and my father's recitations of Robert Frost. I recall studying haiku in fourth grade, writing a free verse ode to football in seventh grade, and of course nobody makes it out of high school without learning a limerick or two, none reprintable here.

Somewhere during this time I began giving my grandmother a sheaf of my original illustrated poems for Christmas each year. Until her death, I was reminded of this every time I walked in her front door, where—despite all the forced rhymes and callow yearning—they hung framed and immortalized on the wall, because that's what grandmas do.

Then came college and the straightforward curriculum of a nursing degree, broken only by required enrollment in a scatter of humanities electives. I signed up for a creative writing course and was caught off guard by how much I enjoyed the poetry segment. This led to reams of angsty verse thumped out on a manual typewriter in my bedroom while listening to *Purple Rain* on garbled cassette. It also led me—after graduation—to write an essay for a local magazine edited by a man named Frank.

Frank recognized early on that my writing style was impaired by cowboy books, naivete, and no doubt Neil Diamond. As an antidote he began handing me poetry books: Sharon Olds, Frank Stanford, Rita Dove, James Wright, Theodore Roethke, Lucille Clifton, Li-Young Lee, Mark Doty . . . on and on. Frank also introduced me to my first poetry reading, and soon I was taking my turn at the open mic, reading poems that weren't really poems but rather navel-centric literary *fartlek* training for the prose marathons to follow.

Eventually I realized (likely while listening to the Dylan Thomas Caedmon Collection) that I wasn't much of a poet. (For starters, I never really shook the Neil Diamond influence.) (Stated without apology and with *Love at the Greek* in the CD changer.) But what a blessing, those poets who persevere: Only this week I reread *shattered sonnets love cards and other off and back handed importunities* by Olena Kalytiak Davis and was amazed again at words being used that way.

There is this idea that poetry must be *gotten*. Admission: I don't get the half of it. But it sure is delicious. Dylan Thomas himself once said he chose words for their taste over their meaning; that works for me. At family reunions my maternal grandfather sat in his recliner and scribbled out rhyming poems about the old days that he would then read aloud to a semicircle audience of cross-legged grandchildren. Doggerel by most standards, those stanzas echo down through our family history even today.

Perhaps the thing about poetry even more than the poetry itself is that we must make time for it. We must surrender our hearts and ears and eyes. Focus less on "getting" it than having it. Just last evening, when the autumnal Midwest was dark and rainy and cold and I was wondering what chance poems have in this loud modern world where words spew from Twitter feeds like clotted soup out a fire hose, I tapped a retweet by the musician Jason Isbell and found myself reading Langston Hughes's "Daybreak in Alabama" on my cell phone and it was like the world split open, which it had.

THE LEAST RAP-LIKE CAT IN THE HOUSE

Two summers ago I stopped to visit a neighbor a couple of corn-fields down the road and there encountered an itinerant rapper, which is the sort of thing that can happen in an age when the catch and release of music is no longer the exclusive purview of cities and coasts and may be committed, yea, even within view of Holsteins.

His name was Andy, although he goes professionally by the name of Astronautalis. He concocted this stage moniker as a callow youth, thinking it sounded spacy, scientific, metaphorically complex, and two or three other things that seemed to be real mind-blowers at the time. Now he shakes his head and says it is a silly name, but in fact he wears it well. (Referring to his cockeyed Shel Silverstein hit, "A Boy Named Sue," Johnny Cash once said you should never record a song unless you're willing to sing it every night for the rest of your life—his tone of voice indicating he learned this *after* the fact.)

I will never get a gig as a paid consultant on the history or present state of rap and its variant subsets (although I welcome any street cred due me for listening to a friend's Kurtis Blow cassette while tearing down and scrubbing milking machines in rural Chippewa County in 1980), but I liked Andy's work immediately upon hearing his album *Pomegranate,* which struck me less as a rap album than brash literature. Filled with painterly images and hybrid rhymes, and salted with historical references, it took me to unexpected places (consider the opening line of "An

Episode of Sparrows": *just as the last of the hay's cut today . . . ,* which caught my ear for the obvious farm boy reasons). Also, it was good typing music. I'm not sure that's what a rapper wants to hear, but there y'go. On many a molasses-brain morning, the martial insistence of "Two Years Before the Mast" has been just the thing to put a kick in the keyboard.

Astronautalis plays all over the world, an endless one-man tour of couches and red-eyes, rapping to hundreds (and occasionally thousands) one night, then a disinterested bartender the next. It's not easy, but Andy's making it. Got his first apartment this year, paying the rent with his craft by hustling his craft. *Face to the forge,* as he puts it in the spoken lines of "Avalanche Patrol."

It is my policy not to overreach in my appreciation, so I did not join the young and fierce people in the front row of last night's show, but settled rather for earplugs and a chair at a table in the back, a wise choice in that even from that distance the speakers stomped my sternum like an anabolic CPR instructor with anger issues.

But the words. The words were good. The ones I recognized, sure, but Astronautalis also does a freestyle segment in which he solicits random words from the crowd and uses them to create a free-flowing rap on the fly. There is an ephemeral electric punch to a performance like this that can be felt only in the instant. I sat quietly in the back and left the fist pumping to others, but I was smiling. Smiling at the ways a chance encounter can lead to a moment like this, when the least rap-like cat in the house feels the energy of the MC and his work and is reminded yet again how sleepy we can become rolling along in a rut up to our hubs, how good it is to put ourselves in the path of new energies, if only to knock ourselves sideways, which, by definition provides a fresh perspective.

MEDITATION SQUIRREL

A guy's gotta do what he can for his brain (to say nothing of his marriage), so I recently agreed to attend a weekend meditation retreat with my wife. "Agreed" is an interesting word here, as I was given the option of not attending, but after passing on the previous seventeen or so, one had a sense that there was more at stake than inner peace.

Through years of hard work, dedication, practice, and personal discovery, my wife has become the yogic equivalent of an acrobatic thought ninja. Over the same course of time I have discovered that if you stack three yoga mats directly on top of each other you can just about take a nap on them. The key is to position them equidistant between the six directions of the universe and about four feet out from the woodstove.

That said, I'm a guy who remains open to alternative ways of thinking (Fleet Farm or Farm & Fleet—who am I to say? Go in peace.) and am totally willing to expand my consciousness (although, again: naps are nice). I also have plenty of opportunity to study my wife, and am fully resolved on whether the world needs more people like me or more people like her—so I'm trying to be more like her.

When we arrived at the yoga studio, I was one of three men in the room, so basically it was like going back to nursing school, only without the embarrassing polyester smock and white shoes.

(For meditation class I wore jeans, a flannel shirt, and gray socks.) (This is what we call "meeting halfway.") (Plus, the world is not ready to see me barefooted in a seafoam green tank top and mid-calf drawstring yoga knickers.)

Right off the bat I caught a break when the instructor said I would be allowed to meditate while sitting upright in a chair. It's not that I can't achieve your classic full lotus position, it's that the end result would be the equivalent of botched bilateral hip replacement. There is the added bonus that I long ago mastered the art of napping while sitting upright in a chair.

The instructor began by playing a DVD featuring a revered Tibetan monk whose brochures I'd seen around the house. He seemed a cheerful and peaceful fellow, although I admit the first thing I thought of when I saw him sitting cross-legged in an armchair was *Hey! Get your feet off the furniture! I just heard Mom pull up!* These are the sort of thoughts that impede your progress along the dharmic arc.

Much of the wisdom the monk shared was of a classically monkish sort (I will need several additional lives and a set of flash cards to gnaw my way through the Four Immeasurables), but there were two very humanizing moments. The first came when—while expanding on the aforementioned Immeasurables—he invoked the phrase *yada-yada*. The second came when he said one of the chief purposes of meditation is to "tame the *monkey-mind*."

I could use some of that. Since I don't wish to insult monkeys, let's just say my mind operates like a nervous squirrel in a roomful of acorn-scented Super Balls. I mean, mostly I like it in there, but there are times I wish we could stay in one gear and just drive, without all the frantic veering and Y-turns. So when the DVD segment concluded and the workshop instructor led us into our first meditation, I put all the jokes on hold and tried my best. The squirrel paused among the Super Balls. I snuck a peek at my wife, only two feet away and a thousand miles ahead of me.

Back in my head, the squirrel raised his paw.

"Yes?" I said.

"Yada-yada," said the squirrel.

"Works for me," I said, and off we went, zigzagging our way down the Eightfold Path.

MONTAIGNE AND ME

Michel de Montaigne has been dead some 423 years now, thus I admire him from afar. Mine is an amateur study of the man, reading him in bits and pieces over the years, often on my phone while sitting in the woods or with a highlighter in the old green chair I inherited from my grandmother. Born into wealth and privilege, Montaigne still managed to be a real overachiever. He began speaking Latin at the age of two, went to college at the age of six, enrolled in law school when he was fourteen, served in the military, held several high-level government positions, hung out with the Pope, and retired at the age of thirty-eight to invent—or at the very least popularize in enduring fashion—the essay as a literary form. Despite this envy-making resumé, one of the chief reasons for Montaigne's enduring popularity (as explicated in Sarah Bakewell's excellent *How to Live: Or a Life of Montaigne in One Question and Twenty Attempts at an Answer*) is his ability to write in such a way that when we read him we recognize ourselves, no matter who we are.

Naturally, I have my own pet Montaigne matchups: He had a kidney stone; I had a kidney stone. (Actually, he had an avalanche of them; I had one. He used them to hone his character and gain insight on the human condition; I popped Toradol and quivered.) He wrote in a castle tower; I write in a room above the garage. He quotes Epicectus from memory; I quote Ray Wylie Hubbard from Google. I say I'm gonna go write in my room over the garage;

Montaigne commissioned an engraved plank declaring that he had "retired to the bosom of the learned virgins."

So it's not a real mirror-image situation.

Here, above all, is why I like Montaigne: He is willing to say "I dunno . . ." He is a paragon of fair-minded uncertainty, whose most familiar coda is *I could be wrong.* As a rural Midwestern former-fundamentalist-Christian white boy I have made some positional and philosophical adjustments in my day (and more to come, I trust, and many hope), but in no case did these changes come about as the result of high-decibel hectoring, public shaming, or a bumper sticker. Following on this, I try to offer anything I write in the spirit of cautious inquiry. In the introduction of *How to Read Montaigne,* Terence Cave points out that Montaigne was prone to "caution and provision," manifested in his regular use of the word "perhaps" and the phrase "it seems to me." I am always caught off guard when I receive communication from readers outraged or hurt by something I've ventured. As if I had donned my ironclad underpants and declared myself the Incontrovertible King of Thinking, when in fact I'm just trying to figure things out while traipsing around clad in the patchy bathrobe of diffidence.

It is Montaigne's spirit of inquiry (in all things—be it Greek philosophy or trouble in the bedroom) and fallibility that recently led me to read Roxane Gay's essay collection *Bad Feminist.* If you read Roxane Gay—I mean really read her, not just yell at her on Twitter—you will find that as with Montaigne, nothing is off the table, whether it's a late-night trip to the bathroom or misogyny in music. If I find myself discomfited by something she has written I probably need to be, and I also notice she is sticking her own neck out. How else are we going to learn? But above all I find Gay embodies that most Montaigne of traits, a willingness to acknowledge her own contradictions—which in turn leads me to think, well, here is a person with whom I might have an actual conversation.

In a world well populated by people busily being really sure of themselves—really sure they are right, and really sure anyone who disagrees is an ingrate dipped in idiocy—I understand we cannot forever spin in our dinghy upon the dithering wishy-wash. At some point we have to make a decision and make a move. But in between, give me Montaigne: *I am free to give myself up to doubt and uncertainty, and to my predominant quality, which is ignorance.*

How else am I gonna learn?

THE SEPTIC TANK GUY

Deep in a dark, dank corner of our basement, which supports our house just fine but is pretty much otherwise useless unless you are conducting a study of fluid dynamics (specifically seep), self-treating your arachnophobia, or into the sport of growing odd things on your rutabagas, there is a red box with a red light and a buzzer that—when triggered—emits a noise similar to that of an army of angry june bugs trapped in a waxed paper factory. As a guy who has carried an ambulance and fire department pager for most of the past twenty-five years, I'm used to things that buzz and deliver bad news, and I'll run toward most trouble and trauma by reflex. But when that red box in the basement buzzes, I run downstairs to hit the silencer, then run back upstairs and phone a man called Phil, because that buzzer is hooked up to the septic tank, and that is not the sort of trouble and trauma I am looking to treat. I have a long record of attempting things for which I have no skills or qualification, but when the phrase "getting in over your head" slides past metaphor and drops into raw sewage, well, it's time to hit the speed dial.

Phil's name isn't Phil, but he took over the business from a guy named Phil, so a lot of people call him Phil, and he's okay with that. I like Phil because he's one of those fellows who just shows up and knows his stuff, and gets down to business, but if the kids want to see how the giant wet vac works, well, he's happy to take the time. Or if I wander over and peer down into the depths, he'll explain how the float valve was hanging up, or show me the scorch marks on the wiring performed by the previous person, who may have understood septics but was a tad undertrained in the administration of electricity.

We live in an age when techno-heads hold the keys to the kingdom, but Phil holds the keys to the chamber pot, and until digital transubstantiation becomes a thing, Phil wins, because even the breezy beautiful people in smartphone ads are contributing to Phil's retirement fund, as it were. "Behold, children," I have been known to say, cautiously leading my tots to the lip of the tank, "a problem not zappable by app!" Should those same children become the next world-surfing digital kajillionaires, I will happily retire aboard their yachts; in the meantime, I have also encouraged them to consider pursuing the alternate fine arts of plumbing and associated materials handling, because what you've got there is steady work.

This time it was the pump, which had given up the ghost after untold decades of worthy service. Phil set it on the lawn and then he and I stood there and looked at it, because that's what you do when something's busted, you stand there and look at it. After all this time it wasn't specifically identifiable as a pump, and in fact what I thought as I stared at the caked lump of it was *Well, there's your mortality right there,* whether it's me, Phil, or the Queen of England.

It was a beautiful sunny day with a touch of breeze. Phil lit a Winston and we visited; a little bit about the weather, a little bit about the business, and an entire cigarette's worth about the state of things in general. Then he carefully stubbed the cigarette out on the concrete cap and placed the butt beside three others. Later, after Phil left, I reset the red box alarm and swung by the tank to check that everything was in order. The new pump was neatly wired, the cap was secure, and the cigarette butts had been swept up and removed, and right there is your master's thesis on honorable work honorably done.

PRINCE

Recently I was working on a book manuscript, and I wrote this:

> Perhaps you failed to guess, but I owe the bulk of my aesthetic construct to Prince Rogers Nelson, circa the movie *Purple Rain,* circa cassette. The film and album were released the summer after I graduated from high school. Come fall, when college was back in session, I had sat solo in the theater watching *Purple Rain* a minimum of four times, worn the hubs off the soundtrack, stocked my bedroom at Grandma's house with purple scarves and fat candles, and scotch-taped fishnet to the drywall above the bed (intended to create shadows of mystery but in reality a most pointless snare). I furthermore spent time snipping words and letters out of old magazines and taping them around the edges of the bureau mirror to re-create Prince's lyrics in the style of a hostage note, phonetic shorthand included (Prince was text message before text message). That very same summer I left Wisconsin to work as a cowboy in Wyoming, made my first trip to Europe, and began experimenting with hair mousse.
>
> All us cosmopolitans gotta start somewhere.

Of course I wrote this having no idea that Prince would be dead within a few weeks. When I heard the news, I posted the excerpt on my blog. It's tricky, commenting publicly about the deaths of famous people. I'm walking a fine line of leveraging someone's very real personal tragedy to draw attention to myself. I'm throwing encomiums at someone I didn't really know. I'm one of millions saying the same thing, or variations on the same thing. None of it one bit of help to the dead man.

Then again, I also wrote this:

> I'm a stocky flat-footed farm boy from Chippewa County, Wisconsin, who can't dance a lick. But Prince in his own purple way set me free. The book I'm working on is about the French philosopher and essayist Montaigne, who once wrote, "I now, and I anon, are two several persons; but whether better, I cannot determine." I think of my young self trying to be Prince, a foolish pursuit on the face of it, but essential at the heart of it, leading as it did to other gracious worlds.

The social media comments that followed my post were heartening. So many people from so many walks of life testifying to how some song, some show, some snippet of film or video held meaning for them in ways we might never suspect.

One commenter was more concise, writing: "Get a life. Really."

Well, sure. There are far grimmer troubles afoot. The fact remains: A very real person did very real work, and it had a very real effect on my life. That doesn't mean I *worshipped* Prince, or thought there was a *perfect* Prince, or that I liked everything he did. Or that my opinions in this instance matter one whit. I'm simply grateful for what he put out there that eased and brightened my clodhopper path.

Get a life?

Did.

Have.

And woven through the blue jeans and flannel and lumpy T-shirts you'll find the thinnest thread of purple.

ROBIN'S-EGG BLUE

Last week my grade-schooler discovered a robin's nest built just three feet off the ground in a short spruce down by the pole barn. There were two eggs in residence and she left them be, choosing instead to tug the family down there by hand, one by one, to see the nest. When I went for my visit the robin was hunkered in place so we observed from a distance, but later when I passed by on my way to the barn for a piece of lumber I noticed the nest was empty and I peeked. The eggs were the usual marvelous blue, a color that always reminds me of Edward Hopper's painting *Seven A.M.,* which draws on a paler version of the hue to impart the lonesome feel of an empty room viewed from an unbridgeable remove. Which is quite a trick, especially when I was only gonna talk about eggs.

Perhaps related to the fact that I am susceptible to sad paintings, there is this grim parental part of me that feels driven to cushion my children's every hope and joy against pending reality. When my daughter first showed me the nest and said she couldn't wait to see the baby robins, I found myself winding up for a speech on the dangers of wind and cowbirds and cats and the miserable uncertainty of life in general, only just as I was opening my big yapper it occurred to me that the neuroses in play here were my own and should remain as such. There will be occasion aplenty for her to learn about life's broken eggs. Still, I found myself chewing over the conundrum of this instinct to guard against hope and joy in order to lessen the impact of darkness and disappointment.

These are the sort of ruminations that prevent me being hired to entertain at children's birthday parties.

Rather than go full existential Eeyore, I chippered up and drew her attention to the construction of the nest. This led to a discussion of the building materials—in this case, dried weeds and pine needles. I told her about one I'd seen woven mostly from horsehair. "And how about the robin that built the nest above my office door last year? Remember that? She used a streamer from your Easter basket."

"Yes," she said, smiling. That nest had been torn apart in a nighttime thunderstorm. The next morning my office steps were stained with yolk and bits of shattered eggshell. When my daughter stopped to visit me after school and spotted the shredded nest and flecks of blue on the ground she'd said, "Ohhh . . . that's sad!"—and then skipped off to play. Reflecting on this memory, it occurs to me perhaps she'll figure out this darkness/lightness thing fine without my dire preemptive speechifying.

At the supper table the night she discovered the nest, she asked, "How many eggs does a robin lay?" I started to reach for the dumb smartphone, then stopped. Just because Google *has* the answer does not mean Google *is* the answer. "I guess you'll just have to see," I said.

And so for the past several days she has trucked straight from the school bus to that nest, then bounded to the house with a full report. So far the clutch has grown to four.

Last night we had a thunderstorm with wind that blew buckets across the yard and left the drive strewn with branches. The nest—and the eggs—survived just fine. For now we're going with hope.

APP-HAPPY

Over there in a corner of my little office above the garage sits a Smith-Corona portable typewriter. It's the manual sort, not electrified, so you really have to hammer at the keys. Writing on that thing is to word processing as logging is to polishing furniture. I use it to bang out a rough draft now and then. I like the rhythm and rumble of it, and the satisfying *ding!* at the end of each line. I also find that the inability to cut-and-paste and revise on the fly helps me maintain forward motion, which is the key to writing and life.

The other handy thing about that Smith-Corona is it predates the Alt key, and no matter how many times per minute I reflexively hit the Caps-Tab combination to check my email and social media, the screen never changes. This forces my focus and also saves on internet usage, which on our dead-end farm is a precious and throttled commodity.

But let's not get all twelve-pound Sears catalog nostalgic here. In the main, I am a fan of electrons and smartphones and apps, especially those that enhance the odds of sustaining successful self-employment while maintaining residence deep in the heartland and ten minutes from an operational feed mill. I've never been what they call "an early adopter," but I think you could call me a "happy adopter." I'm always pleasantly surprised to discover virtual tools I can use—especially of the more fundamental sort.

For instance, very early into the life of my first smartphone, our little family was settling into its first evening's stay in a small lake cabin when a storm knocked out the power. "We need a flashlight app," I joked. Then I checked my new phone's app menu. And there it was. One download, and sixty seconds later my phone was a flashlight and the kids could find their sleeping bags. I couldn't have been more delighted had I suddenly discovered that my phone allowed me to control the Mars rover.

Not long after that, I was working in the chicken coop and found myself in need of a carpenter's level. I own two of them, but they were both down in the pole barn. Again, on a whim, I tapped into the apps and found, yep, a level app. I stood right there with my boots in the you-know-what and downloaded the thing. It came complete with the oblong green bubble, faux wood-grain effects, and illuminated x and y axes, the whole deal. And it worked great. Perhaps the finish carpenters among you would find it unacceptable, but it does the job for a nail-bender like me.

I know there are far more impressive phone features and functions than a flashlight and a level. But they're my favorite type. It's one thing to have a mystery digital toy that can track Grandma's flight from Chicago in real time, or kill digital zombies with the flick of a finger, or allow you to deposit a check in the bank while you're parked in the recliner. This is the sort of magic you expect from an electronic doodad. But to be able to download a tool that will help you rig a roost so the chickens won't all wind up sliding down to the same end? That's technology I can believe in.

There is the argument that Grandpa's wholly tangible wooden level never froze up if you double-tapped it wrong, nor did it require software updates, and it certainly didn't hassle you with pop-up ads. And of course there are some things you simply can't app. A good pair of boots. A pitchfork. A toilet plunger. A quality jackknife (although I suppose a phone-mounted cutting laser isn't out of the question). Also, even as I was typing this I Alt-Tabbed over to my Twitter feed just as a friend tweeted, "Where's my great idea app?" Some things still require old-school gray matter.

My younger daughter was born the same year as the first version of a certain very popular smartphone and has been known to help Dad troubleshoot tech issues. The other day she asked me to show her how to use the typewriter. I set her up, rolled in a sheet of paper, and turned her loose while I went back to work on my laptop.

She had been at it quite a while when she stopped. "Dad?"

"Yes?"

"Does this use a lot of electricity or a lot of internet?"

"Nope. None."

"Well, that's good," she said, and then it was back to *rappety-tackety-tap.*

Readers know I am recursive in my determination to avoid becoming Mr. InMyDay PorchYeller, but as I listened to my app-savvy tot knocking out the alphabet on a WiFi-unenabled antique I was reminded that progress doesn't always take us forward, and soon I ought to take her down to the pole barn and show her how to operate a tangible carpenter's level.

Ding!

FRANCIS AND THE HEAT LIGHTNING

On a blanket-black night in the countryside an illuminated man plays a piano between two oak trees.

I'm so sorry for what I've done . . .

The lyrics warp from his mouth, twisted by a storm-front gust. The distant dark horizon pulses with heat lightning; the clouds turn a shuddering orange. The man leans toward the microphone, his shoulders scarecrow square within a tattered suit coat, and sings into the wind:

. . . and I'm out here all alone.

On the face of it this is sheer frivolity: a costumed man perched at a piano in a barren yard in rural Wisconsin after nightfall in early April, singing a Tom Waits song about being all alone even as he is white-lit by a ring of jury-rigged spotlights, his every move documented by a pair of circling videographers and a handful of crew—to say nothing of a herd of beef cows across the road, last seen huddled at dusk, tails to the pending weather.

But the man is working.

Due to my flat-footed farm boy roots, I am forever trying to reconcile this sort of work with the sort of work done at the wooden end of a pitchfork, or atop a tractor, or with blistered hands. As if work doesn't count unless it produces a pile of something you can stack on a wagon. But I know the story of this artist. Know how he came to be here. How he struck out for New York City on his own. How he lived in the back of a decommissioned mail truck. How he works long night after long night, no matter the presence or absence of the spotlight. His name is Francis. Or part of his name is Francis. He likes some mystery. He told me once, "I built this frame, and within this frame I do the show *I* would want to see."

What I heard there was the word "built." In other words, in light of all the world's ugliness and fear and horror and rent due, the surreal scene before me is *of course* a frivolity, but it is also a product of dedication and perseverance and—if we must talk tangible goods, and from the perspective of the crew on hire this evening—is fungible in the form of groceries, car payments, and—yes—rent due. In other words: *Work.* In fact, my own presence is due to work peripheral to this nocturnal shoot.

The heat lightning is glowing whiter, and the first naked bolts are stitching the sky. Dust swirls in the spotlights. The wind smells like rain. The crew is rushing to get one more take. "Are you good?" asks one of the videographers. "Can you keep going?"

"Yeah, man," says Francis. "I can do this all night."

I like to keep chickens, in part so that I may never completely forget what it is to run a pitchfork. One cannot fix the plumbing with a song, one cannot dance a heart bypass, the poet's pen will rarely adjust your carburetor. But as the singer leans into his song once more, I am grateful for that tenacious, indefatigable, powerfully *frivolous* element of humankind that drives some to stand out there all alone in a frame of their own making, *working,* yes, *working,* facing the distant dark horizon from the center of their own infinitesimal heat lightning flash.

TRANSCENDENCE FROM THE DISCOUNT BIN

Within my telephone there is a song written by a Frenchman 120 years ago. It's a classical piece. From an opera, nonetheless. Specifically it is a symphonic intermezzo (*Just as I thought, Wikipedia!*). Its cultural pedigree should in no way be diminished by the fact that it is digitally ripped from a "Best Of" CD I spotted in a discount bin while making a pit stop during a weeks-long road trip a decade ago. As I recall it was in there with *David Allan Coe: 17 Greatest Hits* and *Legends of Guitar Rock: The 60s, Volume One.*

I bought all three, but let's not get distracted. I'm here to talk about classical music in the classical sense, although I might not be your go-to guy in this respect. My appreciation for classical music is sincere but my appetite is intermittent and my aptitude limited. Nothing better conveys this than purchasing your classical music from a discount bin in "Best Of" format. Then there was the time I read a *New Yorker* essay on the Ring Cycle, got all culturally charged up, went online, and ordered a Wagner CD, managing somehow to choose the one decorated with images of the choppers from *Apocalypse Now.*

That day when I returned to my car, however, and put the CD into the CD Walkman hooked up to the cassette adapter that allowed the erudite tones of orchestral culture to achieve full expression of every nuance the sound system of an '89 Ford Tempo would allow, the music felt cleansing and uplifting. I had also spent the better part of the previous five hundred miles listening to talk radio, so that might have harshed my palate.

The CD knocked around my car for a while, then my bachelor pad, and then wound up in some boxes during a postmarriage move. At some point I uploaded it to my iTunes and it migrated to my phone. Lately I have gotten in the habit, after lunch, of resting my phone on the arm of the old green chair in my room over the garage (where I go to *work,* and therefore must not be disturbed) (*especially* right after lunch) and putting "Méditation" on repeat.

The song was composed by Jules Massenet for his opera *Thaïs,* in which there are tricky interactions between a monk and a hedonistic courtesan. "Méditation" is intended to convey a period of reflection, which comes in handy whenever monks and hedonism meet. I'm sure the tune is lovely in the setting and context intended, but I hereby put my feet up on Grandma's avocado green ottoman and declare it one of my all-time favorite tunes to be appreciated on a sunny afternoon beside an open window. There are a couple of points in which the orchestra winds its way up to a passage of high, clear, wistful solo violin notes, and in that moment—even over thrice-dunked tinny smartphone speakers— it is possible to imagine oneself becoming light as a thin white cloud in the bluest of skies, with a view to the world green and gentle below. I also tend to read the news over lunch, which leads to my understanding the world is filled with horrors and who am I to be in this chair listening to this music in this beautiful, peaceful place? I can't answer that one. I can only report in gratitude that somewhere in that one high, pure passage, if only for a moment, if only in one's cottony head, one can imagine—if not attain—transcendence, and that is a mighty fine thing to dig out of the discount bin.

SAMMI ON REPEAT

By matter of coincidence it is my privilege to work with musicians now and then, many of them much younger than I. At this
stage of my life I'll take whatever youthful spirits I can get, so I
am grateful for their energy. I am also grateful to my daughters,
as by default they keep the old man abreast of the latest vibes
and chart-toppers.

All that said, last night I wound up listening to the late Sammi
Smith, and I want to wish all the young strummers luck.

Born Jewel Fay Smith, Sammi dropped out of school when
she was eleven and was singing in nightclubs by the time she
was twelve. Three years later she married the first of three hus-
bands (the second of which was Willie Nelson's bass player).
I'm tempted to make some wry "that'll do it" comment, but as a
father of daughters and having taken a few unanticipated detours
myself over time, I'll settle for saying you can hear it all in her
voice—smoky, dusky, and worn before its time.

But of course that sound was also what launched her first
giant hit: "Help Me Make It through the Night," a song written
by a janitor named Kris Kristofferson. As I was in first grade at
the time and living in a house where the radio was not played, I
might have heard it emanating from someone's pickup truck at
the feed mill, or a transistor playing in the hardware section of
the Farmer's Store. But by and large I never really picked up on
Sammi Smith until 2005, when the *Oxford American* magazine
published a music issue accompanied by a CD that included a

song by one of my favorite music trivia answers ever ("Hot Smoke and Sassafras," by Bubble Puppy) but also, on Track 22, featured a song called "This Room for Rent" by Sammi Smith. The first time I heard it, I had dropped the CD in the tray while I was doing something else. An album that long, it was maybe an hour before the laser reached the Sammi Smith track, so I wasn't anticipating it, but the moment I heard that world-weary voice deliver those first eighteen words—*this room's for rent so you feel free to turn the key and walk right through the door*—I stopped dead and listened straight through. This was a love song, but a love song busted flat. Everything in it . . . the rattle-trap drums, the imagery (cigarette-scarred tables, empty coffee cups and beer cans on the floor, a woman drying her eyes "on the corner of a scratchy paper towel") but above all Sammi Smith's voice, seasoned dark as the wood of a tavern bar top . . . drives the merciless narrative without once resorting to self-pity or histrionics, simply and steadily relating the tale until the ending, when the whole works leaves the rails like a slow freight train—no screeching, no explosions, just the dead solid end of the line, drive wheels in the dirt and no chance of getting back on track.

From what I've read, beginning to end, Sammi Smith didn't have an easy life, and you can hear it in her voice. In all the songs, even the ones that fall far short of "This Room for Rent." Mine is not to say the beauty of the songs was worth the trouble of her life, which ended at the age of sixty-one. But every now and then when I find my vibe doesn't match what's on the radio or when my young musician friends try to sing sad but come up a bit shallow, I hole up, put Sammi on repeat, and let her sing for the remaining rest of us well-worn sinners.

WITH OPEN EARS

While I enjoy a wide variety of music and feel the richer for it (you never know when a touch of Japanese grindcore is going to hit the spot), by and large my musical tastes are lagged to a bracket of time between when vinyl records were still on their first go-round and the ascension of CDs, which came spinning into my music collection like silver rainbow Frisbees from outer space (I participated in the entire life cycle of the cassette). Thanks to a teenaged daughter and a few friends in the music business, I maintain a passing familiarity with whatever's on the radio or rounding out the top ten streaming services but by and large I am contentedly behind the curve.

Music speaks to us through the filter of our own time and experience. Last week my wife called to say she had pulled to the side of the road in tears because she had made the mistake of listening to "The One Who Knows" while driving the kids to school. From this I take a twofold message: 1) I need to listen to that song, and 2) a guy might oughta schedule a date night. My first favorite song was "Tell Me the Story of Jesus," in part because of the soothing melody, and in part because it was the first song in the church hymnbook and thus easily located by the preschool me. The first two popular songs I recall wanting to hear over and over were Pete Seeger's "Riding in My Car" and Johnny Cash's "A Boy Named Sue." A disparate pair, but I associate both with the dusty crackles emanating from our portable phonograph with the plastic handle, and assume I fancied them for their sing-along properties. Somewhere along the adolescent line Herb Alpert's *Whipped Cream and Other Delights* became a signal favorite, although this was a fascination based primarily on the cover art. In my teen years I was deep into pop, if such a thing was possible, and during college I attended numerous screenings of *Purple Rain* and tried to be just like Prince, which presented its own specific challenges. To this day his influence on me is profound if not obvious. Right along the same time, I discovered Waylon Jennings on an eight-track, and somewhere between "When Doves Cry" and "Ramblin' Man" I began to locate my shifting center.

I also went through a pusillanimous stage in which I felt it necessary to disparage music that fell short of my self-righteous definitions of "good" and "bad." I still have my opinions but have come to feel that within the grand scheme of things my energy is better focused elsewhere, to say nothing of inward. These days I try to listen with a more open ear. In part I grew out of this stage when a friend told me, "There are no guilty pleasures—only pleasures." There are times when my teenager shares her latest favorite and I actually resonate with it—same goes with the younger child. Then again I'm not gonna be the flat-footed bald dad pretending I totally get the latest YouTube fiddle-dee-dee (although we have had more than one sit-down where we work-shopped certain lyrics in discussions addressing both content and context), and I also recently made a mixtape (okay, a mix-CD) for the tots that includes Patsy Cline, Mahalia Jackson, Neko Case, Sister Rosetta Tharpe, and Aretha. R-E-S-P-E-C-T, I said, and turned it up.

It's nice to hit that stage of life where you enjoy some of the old music, some of the new music, and above all are simply happy there is music. The most recent artist who has moved me in a way I've not felt moved in a while is Sturgill Simpson. I read an interview recently where someone suggested he could be the voice of a new generation of country music. He demurred, and furthermore rejected the implication that he might denigrate the current state of the genre. Rather, he said, we oughta "just get in where you fit in."

Yep.

THE BIG BLUE TENT

Up there in Bayfield County they're rolling canvas. The breezes on Mount Ashwabay—located between Washburn and Bayfield—have been blowing cool lately, the leaves that sprang in spring as green and tender as butter lettuce are showing other colors and will soon be brown and crackling on the ground, and the Lake Superior Big Top Chautauqua tent is once again being struck and stowed.

That makes thirty years now.

I was a latecomer to the tent when I bought two tickets to see a Greg Brown concert there over a decade ago. Nowadays I have the opportunity to stand on the stage a time or two over the course of the season, sing a few songs, tell a few stories, and then wander around back and slip through a tent flap to watch the rest of the show from over behind the sound board. I also have the privilege of hosting a radio show featuring Big Top performances. But I am still—above all—a guest: Guest of the founders, guest of the sponsors, guest of the volunteers who really run the show, and guest of the guests, some of whom have been attending performances from day one.

Despite my lifelong Wisconsin residency, for a farmland flatlander like me the trip to Bayfield County is always a fresh revelation about the segments of our state that are more than cows and cornfields. When I visited last weekend, Lake Superior was at its preautumnal finest: crisply blue beneath clear skies and kissed by just enough wind to raise a sparkle from the sun.

The shoreline was still green and rounded with trees (the same shoreline will still be stunning but starker come winter when the deciduous trees stand stripped within the pines and the ice is in) and the Apostle Islands were arranged along the blue horizon. This recollection leads me to recommend a Lake Superior Big Top Chautauqua preshow ritual I wrote up some time ago should you ever attend and time, health, and the weather allow it:

> If you have the desire and constitution, I recommend you arrive early and hike to the top of Mount Ashwabay. Don't look back until you're all the way up there where the skiers unload from the lift. Then turn, and you will see the picture I try to paint every single time I introduce Tent Show Radio: the tent, plopped high atop the land like an Alice in Wonderland pearl-gray-and-blue-striped mushroom, a benevolent psychedelic aberration amidst swathes of verdant green sloping to a backdrop of Great Lakes blue, the distant water dappled by a scatter of treasured islands.

Later then, when the houselights are down and the stage lights are up and you are gathered together with all the others watching the show, you will be able to put your position in universal context. To perform your own sort of global positioning.

But this will have to wait for next year. Summer is in the rearview mirror (this is no reason to stop driving north—on behalf of our tourist-dependent neighbors up that way, let's keep our fingers crossed for a snowful winter and optimum ice cave conditions), the canvas is stashed, and for now the music and laughter will exist only in memory and playback. But soon you will have worn another quarter-inch off your snow shovel blade, the calendar will flip to May, and up on Mount Ashwabay they'll unroll that canvas beneath the spring sun and pitch the Big Top Chautauqua into its fourth decade.

BASEBALL, BRIEFLY

I write this having just returned from an afternoon spent watching my nephew play his final Little League baseball game of the year. There were sacrifices involved, and not only of the bunt and fly variety: the Packers were playing simultaneously, and there were a lot of grown-ups wearing earbuds and furtively refreshing their smartphones between at-bats. I myself availed myself of an update now and then, although the fact that I had forgotten my reading glasses forced me to hold the phone out in front of me at a distance not easily disguised. I pretended it was a speed gun and I was clocking pitches.

It was a glorious day to look over a ball field. The sun flew high and bright in a clear blue sky, the grounds were flanked by trees beginning their full-bore autumnal blaze, and the breeze was light. The only adverse elements manifested in the form of last-ditch warm-weather insects: the occasional persistent wasp in a toddler's yogurt cup and intermittent incoming lady beetles, which are essentially airborne popcorn hulls that stink and bite. Both were inconveniences easily endured in light of the dark, frozen months to come.

The previous evening, my father-in-law and I had enjoyed watching a professional baseball playoff game together. It provided context for the more callow contests unfolding before us today. Fanwise, instead of full-throated thousands, you had the sparser encouragements of whoever got assigned to drive the van to a rural baseball field on a Packers game day. And whereas last night on the high-def television the bats cracked and the leather popped and even the errors happened in a flash, here you had the uncertainty of fielders faced with more than one base runner, the wood-splitter swings at pitches passing a good foot overhead, the dreamers otherwise occupied while an opponent stole one base—and then two. Alternatively, you also saw the joy when the fly ball landed in the glove and stayed there, or when the aluminum bat gave out with a resonant *ping* and the ball sailed beyond the infield and dropped to safety in an unoccupied green patch of outfield, or when the kid who ran like he was forcing his way through a vat of pudding launched himself into what seemed like a five-minute slide and looked up to see the ump signaling him safe.

I only played baseball once. I was on the high school track team and running laps when the baseball coach called my name from the field adjacent. I jogged over. It turned out the team was shorthanded and needed someone to bat and run. My heart leapt: Perhaps I was a baseball savant! A phenom, discovered by chance while training for the two-mile! They would recount the story years from now when I hit a walk-off homer to win the World Series.

I grabbed a bat and dug in. The pitcher reared back and threw. The ball smacked me in the ribs. I wobbled to first and took a lead. The pitcher spun and threw to first. Out. The baseball coach thanked me and sent me back to the track.

There were disappointments at the games today. Strikeouts, missed balls, lopsided scoreboards, slumped shoulders. But to all those youngsters who wound up in the "L" column, or had a tough day at the plate, consider my lifetime baseball statistics: *Hit by pitch. Picked off first. Retired.* Compared to me, you are all winners.

SO LONG SUMMER

This morning a warm rain is falling and outside my window the back forty looks heavy green in the low light, but when the sun comes out it will highlight all the orange and yellow leaves that will soon enjoy their brief majority. When I went out to feed the chickens a hen was waiting for me outside the gate, an escapee who had failed to find her way back inside the fence the night previous. She was damp and discomfited as I dropped her back within the perimeter, but quickly tucked into the feed pan. Chickens do not dwell on the past.

Were that true for me.

I'm better than I used to be. Having crossed the fifty-year yard line, I'm as susceptible as the next person to fond reminiscence and the temptations of revisitation and regurgitation as a substitute for facing the future. Or *encouraging* the future. My demeanor is a perpetual minute-by-minute work in progress, but one of the things I've really been focusing on lately is the way folks seem to take one of two turns as they age: some dig their heels in and make themselves as wide as possible so as to hold back the tide; others keep moving forward while reenergizing themselves on the power of the young and the new. Somewhere in there is the balance, and I'm nowhere near to achieving it, but lately am leaning toward the second path. And for the record, I am talking about trying new thoughts and ideas as opposed to getting a sporty car or a new hairstyle. Regarding the former, I prefer old pickups; regarding the latter, the options simply aren't there.

In fact, I think I am far less maudlin about my memories these days than I was at the age of, say, eighteen, which is a wry irony. Lo, the poems I wrote over the long-lost loves of my hallowed junior year. Such word syrup. It is encouraging, I think, that here in early autumn—the glide path season terminating in winter— I can gaze out the window at the last deep green and anticipate the falling leaves without feeling compelled to pull out the ol' fountain pen of despair, charge it with the tears of yearning, and scribble out a half-baked meditation on evanescence (the thing, not the band, you whippersnappers). Rather, one looks toward the empty chicken run and realizes even a chicken has sense enough to get in out of the rain, so why don't we just get back to work?

And yet as our hemisphere enters the time of turning its shoulder to the sun, I am not impervious: On a cool autumn day when my elder daughter was four years old I found her sitting in her backyard rope swing, disconsolately sobbing. Between deep breaths she told me she was sad about the falling leaves. I said something about autumn bringing us new and pretty colors. This only refreshed her tears, and she exclaimed, "But I want summer to be here every day!"

Today she is a teenager taller than I and just got asked to homecoming. I couldn't be happier for her . . . even as I wish summer could be here every day.

GOING FOR A RUN

I just finished a four-mile run. Let me stop right there in my sweaty shirt and declare: the word *run* in this case is being misused to the point of prevarication. There was a time a long time ago when I ran a mile in under five minutes. Subsequently, fancying myself a bit of a gazelle, I grew my hair long so it would flow in the wind, bought a pair of multicolored running tights, and took to the streets like the sweet Norwegian wind. Fast-forward a few decades and what you've got now is an overgrown flat-footed balding wombat stumping over hill and dale with gravel in his socks.

Glad I got out there today, though. It was one of those country calendar afternoons, with the landscape as deep green as it gets, the sky blue but for a few artfully placed cloud-puffs passing high above a canvas of treetops clustered dense as broccoli, and sparrows chipping and chittering from a farmyard as I passed. Across the ditch, rows of round bales sat curing in the sun, giving off an aroma that brought to mind the whole-leaf chew the old farmers dipped down at the feed mill when I was a boy. Beefers grazed placidly in the valley below.

That farm is a holdout. It's not the only one, but things continue to change out here. At night we can see the lights of the mall. There are apartments beside the livestock sale barn. And today as I chugged down our hill I met a semi hauling an earth-mover, the advance guard of a construction crew set to raise a new house on some adjacent acreage. And in another sure sign of influx, I see more and more joggers out and about. Many of them have earbuds jammed in place and run with the flow of traffic. I interpret this to mean that we as a nation are no longer teaching basic survival skills. I've said it before, and I'll say it again (again): Once you hit forty, you spend every waking day resisting the urge to burn up the rest of your life yelling at anyone who comes within forty feet of your metaphorical porch.

Right at the end of my jog (rhymes with *slog*), my breathing rate became such that it occurred to me to wonder whatever happened to the whole oxygen bar craze. I know it never really caught on in Chippewa County. In fact, even as a nonsmoking teetotaler, I still like it when I pass on the sidewalk beside a small-town bar on a sunny afternoon and catch a whiff of stale smoke and darkness through the screen. As with the curing hay, it allows me to visit—but not stay parked—in another time.

As I turned for the final climb up the steep dead-end road leading home—and alongside the property where the new house will go—I observed a thick clump of brush and was reminded that when my daughter went in there to retrieve the hub cap that spun off our van sometime last winter, she discovered the foundation of a long-abandoned house. It was a helpful tempering reminder that things come and things go. I looked toward the top of the hill, drew a deep and determined breath—and walked the rest of the way.

OUT IN THE COLD

There is this moment when the chickadees approach in such a rush that I think of them not as a flock, but as a *hustle* of chickadees. A dozen or more, landing in the brush and branches all around my head and shoulders, in so close I can hear the *flirrrr* of their wings, the scrape of their talons on the birch bark, and the *peck-peck* of their beaks like specks of sand sprinkled over dry leaves.

Temperatures were on the upswing. The snow, fallen only for a few days, was melting, and all along the bottom side the branches were hung with water droplets. When the chickadees came swarming, featherweights though they were, their activity was enough to shake loose a small rain over my head and shoulders.

Each year come late fall I spend the better part of a week in the woods. This time outdoors serves more than one purpose, the most fundamental being venison chops. But above all it serves a necessary reset. There is a lot of thinking (and sometimes naps, but let us remain philosophical), and not all of it comfortable. I have long held that for all its soothing and restorative potential, nature's true power lies in making us feel deeply vulnerable. Inescapably mortal.

Brief.

Later in the week I sat on a ridge in the predawn dark. The wind was really only a breeze, but when I shone a light on our old mercury thermometer before leaving the yard, the crown of the meniscus had ducked below zero, so even the lightest puff of air felt scabrous; my cheeks were stiff and my whiskers were clotted with icy beads of exhaled moisture (and other, but let's move on—it is difficult to render poetic the snotsicle). Thinking I saw movement against the far side of the valley, I strained to see, only to be faced with the freezer breeze against my corneas. If you have tried this, you know my eyes watered up and spilled over, and everything went to a blur. Emotion doesn't enter into it; this is simply the body responding to the forces of nature that rule us, no matter if you do have a smartphone in your pocket.

In time the eastern horizon lightened but did not brighten; a thick batt of clouds overlaid all visible sky. At sunrise the star itself did not show, but through some unseen, subhorizon break a vast wash of storybook rose leaked through and ruddied up the overcast underbelly in a broad, fan-shaped wash. In a short minute, the red receded, thinning out and going pale and drawing back within itself, and in moments the sky was simply gray again, and perhaps the moral of that story was *this whole works is on the clock.*

Nature provides its comforts. But I value it most for reseeding my unease. For the way it knocks a wobble into my habits and certitudes. The click of one dead goldenrod stem against the other presages my own dry bones. I spend a handful of the short, dark, frozen days—leading up, as they do, to the season of resolutions—staring at the world through a crisscross tangle of leafless aspen slashings or a stand of sumac stripped and shivering in nothing but dark-blooded stocking caps and find myself feeling fragile, a useful state in that it may lead me to step more carefully upon reentry.

One evening late in my November sojourn it began to snow at dusk. I sat until I could see the world in nothing but black and white. The forest was stock-still, so frozen I could hear the sound of snowflakes striking the parchment oak leaves like sprinkled sand, and now I was back to remembering the chickadees. This brought to mind the idea of circles (one of your more obvious and well-worn nature motifs, but no less relevant for it), and then from far off I heard the wash of the interstate, all the back-and-forth hustle its own sort of circle, and I thought, *Well, I'll just stay here until it's completely dark.*

THE WAY THINGS ARE

My neighbor Tom didn't send out any Christmas cards this year. He warned everyone ahead of time that's how it would be. Arlene always sent the cards, he says. About seventy-five of them. He and Arlene were married sixty years. This would be Tom's first Christmas without her.

We were sitting at Tom's dining room table. Christmas was about a week out. Mister Bigshot and Oscar Underfoot—Tom's two cats—were lazing on a stack of magazines and Cassidy the three-legged dog was at our feet angling for a belly scratch. I can't speak for Tom, but Arlene's absence was its own presence.

We had some quiet words about that, and Tom looked off into the middle distance for a moment the way someone does when they haven't quite figured out where to put something, but then he squared up and drew my attention to a pair of miniature fully firing cannons he was fine-tuning (they were set up on the table beside the lazing cats), and when I told him we'd lost a bunch of chickens to a varmint he told me about the time his ma went after a chicken-killing weasel with a pitchfork, and that led him to the story about the time she similarly skewered a rabid skunk, and he just shook his head, saying they never figured out how she managed to avoid getting sprayed, and then since it had been below zero much of the past week he segued into telling me about a stretch way back when it stayed so cold so long frost formed along the baseboards of the living room, and that led him to relive the night in the 1940s when it was forty-five

235

below and he took his convertible to town and the cold left the bias-ply tires flat on one side, and at this point he did a fine impersonation of a man driving a convertible at forty-five below with four squared-off tires.

Point being, this was not a mournful visit. The business about the Christmas cards was simply matter-of-fact. The way things are now.

I headed home. The heater in my own plow truck was blowing good and warm, so I took it easy. The houses along the road between Tom's place and mine triggered memories of blessings received in the year just passed: my costumed daughters fishing through a bowl of Halloween candy offered by the retired husband and wife at the house on the corner, the neighbor who brought his John Deere sickle mower up the hill and cut my oats in July when I had to head off on book tour, the farmer who gives us milk when we ask, the couple with whom we trade babysitting and chauffeuring, and Denny and Linda at the bottom of the hill who take good care of our chickens when we're traveling. Even the one house where I knew there had been some trouble was a reminder to comfort the afflicted, because you never know when you're going to need—as the singer/songwriter Mary Gauthier puts it—*a little mercy now.*

When I got home I found a plastic clamshell of rosettes on the kitchen counter. The sickle-mower neighbor and his fellow congregants make them every Christmas down the road at St. Raymond's, and he always drops off a batch. Each rosette is deep-fried to the far side of golden, then hand-dusted with sugar. Should I ever commit to eating myself to death, those rosettes will be my weapon of choice, and I will go happy.

There's a spot right past our chicken coop where you can stand and see Tom's place. His house is hidden by a ridge, but you know it's in there, cradled in the hollow. Long after the plow truck had cooled to single digits, I went out to close up the chicken coop. I paused and looked out over the valley Tom's way. I was thinking I'd like to be able to put a ribbon on things sometimes.

Tuck the year in a neat little box and wrap it up. But life—while we have it—is perpetual and asymmetrical. Among the many gifts Tom has given me is the idea that we pull what we can from the slipstream—the memory of a kindness done, a moment shared, a new old story told, the glorious annual overdose of rosettes—and rather than mourn the Christmas card not coming, give thanks for what we have and for what we have been given.

For the way things are now.

GRATITUDE

It happens that this essay is being composed in the waning days of December, and thus on the cusp of a new year. I cannot anticipate the state of our hearts as we meet in this moment, but I choose for my subject a word I owe more study whatever may transpire after I type it: gratitude.

Gratitude. Such a lovely word. Humble and warm. Humble, because it's not a word you use if you think you did everything yourself. Humble, because no matter how hard you did work at whatever it is you're grateful for, you know—and more importantly, acknowledge—there was some luck involved. Warm, because gratitude is not compatible with a cold soul. Warm, because gratitude radiates, like the gentle rays of a heart-sized sun. Gratitude goes softly out and does good works—which generate more gratitude. Gratitude is renewable energy.

Gratitude, because to offer anything less would be to ignore all privilege. The privilege of existence. The privilege of health. The privilege of privilege. And now we are back at humility—or ought to be.

Gratitude, because the world is awash with the sour surf of opposing sentiments.

Gratitude, for those who show us the same.

Gratitude, even in grumpiness. Which is to say I am not talking all hosannas, hugs, and puppies here, I am talking about perspective and preponderance and relativity and a sideways glance into the cosmic mirror, where behind me I spy millions of souls who would give all they own for just one of my disappointing Tuesdays. Gratitude as my moral duty.

Gratitude, because it's so easy. A note. A word. You don't even have to talk. Gratitude can be soundless. You can speak it with your eyes. Share it with a smile. Weave it into your works. You can kneel down and offer it up.

Gratitude. A triple-syllabic salutation to the six directions, whichever way you're pointing. The echoes go on and on. The echoes are gratitude returning. There is the idea among psychologists that gratitude can be cultivated. Put it out there and it comes back to you.

Gratitude as a practice. As an intentional act. Gratitude in the form of reflection. A quiet moment. A look back.

Gratitude, not as obligation but as celebration.

Gratitude, with our loved ones in mind. The ones who suffer our ingratitudes with grace, and that grace yet another reason for gratitude. Grace: cousin and catalyst to gratitude.

Gratitude, because as this year—or this day, or this hour, or this moment—draws to a close I am reminded it was another year granted, not guaranteed, and therefore not *taken* for granted.

Gratitude, no matter the season.

Gratitude.

ACKNOWLEDGMENTS

My family, for love and material, kitchen-table fact-checking, and above all, forbearance. My gratitude extends across generations.

My neighbors, neighborly beyond all requirement.

Alissa Freeberg, for international assistance.

Blakeley Beatty, for booking it.

Kate, Kathy, Kristin, Halley, and Elizabeth at the Wisconsin Historical Society Press.

John and Beth at the *Wisconsin State Journal*.

Lisa and Berni at ICM.

TFD and Emergicare for balance.

ABOUT THE AUTHOR

Michael Perry is the *New York Times* bestselling author of numerous books, including *Population: 485, Truck: A Love Story,* and *The Jesus Cow.* His live humor recordings include *Never Stand Behind a Sneezing Cow* and *The Clodhopper Monologues.* He lives in rural Wisconsin with his wife and daughters and is privileged to serve as a first responder with the local fire department. He can be found online at www.sneezingcow.com.